Grounded Theory

POCKET GUIDES TO
SOCIAL WORK RESEARCH METHODS

Series Editor
Tony Tripodi, DSW
Professor Emeritus, Ohio State University

Determining Sample Size
Balancing Power, Precision, and Practicality
Patrick Dattalo

Preparing Research Articles
Bruce A. Thyer

Systematic Reviews and Meta-Analysis
Julia H. Littell, Jacqueline Corcoran,
and Vijayan Pillai

Historical Research
Elizabeth Ann Danto

Confirmatory Factor Analysis
Donna Harrington

Randomized Controlled Trials
Design and Implementation for
Community-Based Psychosocial
Interventions
Phyllis Solomon, Mary M. Cavanaugh,
and Jeffrey Draine

Needs Assessment
David Royse, Michele Staton-Tindall,
Karen Badger, and J. Matthew Webster

Multiple Regression with Discrete
Dependent Variables
John G. Orme and
Terri Combs-Orme

Developing Cross-Cultural Measurement
Thanh V. Tran

Intervention Research
Developing Social Programs
Mark W. Fraser, Jack M. Richman,
Maeda J. Galinsky, and Steven H. Day

Developing and Validating Rapid
Assessment Instruments
Neil Abell, David W. Springer, and
Akihito Kamata

Clinical Data-Mining
Integrating Practice and Research
Irwin Epstein

Strategies to Approximate Random
Sampling and Assignment
Patrick Dattalo

Analyzing Single System
Design Data
William R. Nugent

Survival Analysis
Shenyang Guo

The Dissertation
From Beginning to End
Peter Lyons and Howard J. Doueck

Cross-Cultural Research
Jorge Delva, Paula Allen-Meares, and
Sandra L. Momper

Secondary Data Analysis
Thomas P. Vartanian

Narrative Inquiry
Kathleen Wells

Structural Equation Modeling
Natasha K. Bowen and
Shenyang Guo

Finding and Evaluating
Evidence
Systematic Reviews and
Evidence-Based Practice
Denise E. Bronson and
Tamara S. Davis

Policy Creation and Evaluation
Understanding Welfare Reform
in the United States
Richard Hoefer

Systematic Synthesis of Qualitative
Research
Michael Saini and Aron Shlonsky

Quasi-Experimental Research Designs
Bruce A. Thyer

Grounded Theory
Julianne S. Oktay

JULIANNE S. OKTAY

Grounded Theory

OXFORD
UNIVERSITY PRESS

OXFORD

UNIVERSITY PRESS

Oxford University Press, Inc., publishes works that further
Oxford University's objective of excellence
in research, scholarship, and education

Oxford   New York
Auckland   Cape Town   Dar es Salaam   Hong Kong   Karachi
Kuala Lumpur   Madrid   Melbourne   Mexico City   Nairobi
New Delhi   Shanghai   Taipei   Toronto

With offices in
Argentina   Austria   Brazil   Chile   Czech Republic   France   Greece
Guatemala   Hungary   Italy   Japan   Poland   Portugal   Singapore
South Korea   Switzerland   Thailand   Turkey   Ukraine   Vietnam

Published by Oxford University Press, Inc.
198 Madison Avenue, New York, New York 10016
www.oup.com

Oxford is a registered trademark of Oxford University Press

Library of Congress Cataloging-in-Publication Data
Oktay, Julianne S.
Grounded theory / Julianne S. Oktay.
p. cm. — (Pocket guides to social work research methods)
Includes bibliographical references and index.
ISBN 978-0-19-975369-7
1. Grounded theory. 2. Social service—Research—Methodology. I. Title.
H61.24.O48 2012
361.3072—dc23
2011036800

Printed in the USA on acid-free paper

To my mother, Nadine Shaberman (1914–2010).
A true social worker—both in her profession and in her life.

Preface

Grounded theory, one of the oldest forms of qualitative research, has much to offer to the social work profession today. Although it has been widely used in social work research, it is still often misunderstood and its potential remains unfulfilled. Unfortunately, grounded theory, and theory development in general, has not been included in the active debates in the field today about the relationship between practice and research. The goal of this pocket guide is to provide social work researchers with an understanding of the grounded theory method, how it has developed, its theoretical assumptions, and how to distinguish grounded theory studies from other qualitative methods. The pocket guide provides examples of grounded theory research in the social work field (exemplars), and describes the grounded theory method so that social work researchers will be able to better understand and evaluate grounded theory studies, to conduct grounded theory studies, and to appropriately describe their own research.

HOW I DISCOVERED GROUNDED THEORY AND CAME TO WRITE THIS BOOK

I received a PhD in Sociology and Social Work at the University of Michigan in 1974. At that time, "research" meant "survey research."

Qualitative research was not even on the radar, except for occasional derogative references to the "stuff they do in Chicago." I absorbed this culture, and after graduating, I conducted several quantitative studies, mostly in the field of aging. At the end of these studies, I often felt that while I had answered my carefully constructed research questions, I had learned little about the truly important questions. Frustrated, I ended up with more questions than I had at the start.

When Carolyn Walter came to the social work school where I was teaching, we quickly became friends. Carolyn had recently completed a qualitative dissertation on mothering and women's life course development. I was amazed. "You can do that?!?" This was a topic I knew about, not from research, but from life experience. I was a feminist, but had not applied feminist ideas to my own work. Recently tenured, I felt free to try something different. Carolyn and I worked together on a project that combined our two fields: "women in the life course" and "health." We did a qualitative study on breast cancer in the life course (Oktay & Walter, 1991), and it changed my life. Not only did I enjoy doing the qualitative interviews and data analysis, but I also felt more confidence in the validity of the results than I ever felt in my quantitative studies. I began to study qualitative methods, taking several courses, attending conferences, and doing lots of reading. When I began doing qualitative research, I was not aware of the different types of qualitative research, and used a generic model. Over time it became increasingly important to identify with one of the qualitative traditions. I realized that grounded theory was very compatible with my worldview and the methodology I had been using. I more consciously used a grounded theory model in doing a second qualitative study, with funding from an R03 from the National Cancer Institute on daughters of women with breast cancer (Oktay, 2003, 2005).

As my interest and enthusiasm for qualitative methods grew, I introduced an elective course to the doctoral program at my school, which I taught for many years. In 2009, I introduced a new, advanced qualitative seminar on data analysis focusing on grounded theory. This was designed for students who were ready to begin data gathering and analysis for dissertations or class projects. I often wished that I had had a seminar, similar to the one described by the students of Glaser and Strauss, to teach me and support me when doing my research. I designed the advanced seminar to serve this purpose for doctoral students in our program. The seminar focused primarily on grounded theory. By this time, I had supervised a number of students who used qualitative methods or grounded theory in their dissertations. I used this experience in developing the new seminar.

This volume is based on my seminar, which I have now taught three times. I have had wonderful students who have taught me much more than I have taught them! It was only when I began developing the seminar that I recognized the importance of the common roots of social work and symbolic interactionism (the theory that grounded theory is based on). The more I learned more about grounded theory, the more I came to recognize the potential of this method for social work. I hope that the pocket guide will make more social work researchers aware of this method and what it can offer to our profession.

I do not consider myself an expert in grounded theory. Most grounded theory textbook authors today were students of Strauss or Glaser. I am "self-taught," and I am the first to admit that I have made many mistakes in my effort to put the method into practice. I see myself more like an art lover than an artist. I developed this pocket guide to help those who are not in institutions where they can get a strong background in grounded theory research and analysis. The pocket guide is written primarily for doctoral students in social work, but it should also be of value to researchers who are new to grounded theory, and to those in other fields that also have a practice focus. As a pocket guide, it is designed to serve as a basic introduction to the grounded theory method, as well as a practical guide to how to conduct this type of research.

OVERVIEW

The first two chapters provide a basic introduction to grounded theory and its potential for social work. I begin Chapter 1 with an invitation to the reader to learn about the method, its roots, and its development. I emphasize the particular compatibility grounded theory has for the social work profession. I introduce three exemplar social work grounded theory studies to illustrate the grounded theory method, and to show how it can be used in social work and related fields. This chapter also includes an introduction to the theory of symbolic interactionism, because its ideas are central to an understanding of grounded theory.

Finally, I introduce the basic characteristics and key components of the grounded theory method, how it has evolved since the late 1960s.

In Chapter 2, I address the researcher who is considering whether grounded theory is appropriate for his or her study by showing how the basic characteristics and key components of grounded theory impact study design and the choice of study population. To clarify the basic processes used in grounded theory research, I use the three exemplar studies to illustrate each of these components. With doctoral students in mind, I also show how to develop a research proposal using grounded theory.

In Chapters 3 and 4 I show how to conduct a grounded theory study, emphasizing the coding process. Chapter 3 focuses on the use of open coding to begin to identify concepts from raw data, to develop these concepts by identifying their dimensions and properties, and to consolidate concepts into larger categories. I stress the importance of writing memos at this early stage of analysis and show how open coding and memoing further the use of the "constant comparative" method and theoretical sampling. This moves the analysis toward theory building. Chapter 4 introduces the concepts of axial coding and selective coding, the final stage of grounded theory coding. I present a variety of techniques to stimulate creative thinking in the later stages of coding.

Chapter 5 addresses ideas of quality in classic and newer versions of grounded theory. In grounded theory, credibility is related both to the application of the grounded theory method and the theory that is produced. I emphasize that applicability to practice is key. I provide some detail on Glaser and Strauss's vision of the theory being tested in the field by practitioners, and adapted to different settings, because this aspect of grounded theory has been largely overlooked. However, it is of special importance to a practice field like social work.

In Chapter 6, I consider grounded theory in light of a variety of recent developments in social work research, with an eye to possible future developments. I discuss why it is sometimes difficult to conduct a grounded theory study today, and consider what to do when it is impractical to apply the grounded theory method. I briefly consider ethical and IRB issues in grounded theory research, the practical considerations of publishing formats, the use of computer software programs, and mixed-method research. I also introduce "formal grounded theory," the grounded theory model for synthesizing qualitative studies, because of recent interest in qualitative meta-synthesis.

Throughout the pocket guide, I use the three exemplar grounded theory studies from the social work literature to illustrate grounded theory methods. I strongly advise any reader of this guide to read and study these three studies as you use the pocket guide. Each chapter in the pocket guide ends with several exercises designed to help the student apply the chapter contents to his or her own work.

In grounded theory, I have found a method that brings together theory, research, and practice. I love doing grounded theory, reading good grounded theory studies, and helping students to conduct grounded theory studies themselves. In this volume, I hope to convey my enthusiasm, and to introduce others to this method that is so promising to social work today.

One thing that helps me keep focused is by remembering that many great thinkers have emphasized the importance of the experience-based theory building that is built into the grounded theory approach. For example, Kant spoke of the experience as the basis of all knowledge, saying: "There can be no doubt that all our knowledge begins with experience." Einstein emphasized the importance of creativity to science: "To raise new questions, new possibilities, to regard old problems from a new angle, requires creative imagination and marks real advance in science." And even Yogi Berra saw the importance of grounding theory in practice, famously saying: "In theory, there is no difference between theory and practice. In practice, there is."

Acknowledgments

First, I want to thank all of my students who have helped me not only to better understand grounded theory but also how to help others learn it. I especially want to thank Eunice Park Lee and Marlene Matarese, who generously allowed me to use their work to illustrate important grounded theory techniques. I served as chair for Eunice's doctoral dissertation, and Marlene was a student in the seminar I described above. Their work is ideal for this pocket guide, because it illustrates the grounded theory process in a way that usually cannot be seen in published work. I also want to thank the authors of the three exemplar studies that I used to illustrate the grounded theory method. The works of Ramona Alaggia, Kim Anderson, Fran Danis, and Miu Yan strengthened the volume immeasurably and provided critical ties to social work literature. Special thanks are due to Andrea Jones, currently a PhD student at the University of Maryland, who helped me with the references and the glossary. Her cheerful and quick responsiveness was most appreciated when I got overwhelmed with the many tasks involved in getting the manuscript "out the door." Even more important was her enthusiasm for the book and its potential value to doctoral students. Finally, I express my deep gratitude to Rebecca Sander, whose thoughtful, intelligent comments on the manuscript were invaluable. Becki helped immeasurably by

reading the manuscript when it was barely intelligible and raising important questions that helped me to find both direction and voice. I am
grateful to the book's reviewers, for their excellent suggestions and comments on the book proposal and the first draft of the manuscript. Nicholas
Liu at Oxford University Press was delightful to work with – always
responsive and forgiving of my many missed deadlines. I also want to
acknowledge the inspiration provided by Anselm Strauss, Barney Glaser,
George Herbert Mead, and Jane Addams. Finally, I want to thank Irwin
Epstein for writing a pocket guide (Epstein, 2010) that is open, honest,
and helpful. By sharing his experiences and speaking directly to students,
Epstein's work encouraged me to share my own experiences, rather than
writing from "on high" as an EXPERT.

Finally, I thank my family for being so loving, patient, and supportive. During the time I was writing this book, my mother passed away,
after a long, slow decline with Alzheimer's disease. I especially want to
thank my sister, Susan Shaberman, for her loving care of my mother
during this period. Although I was often distracted with worry and sadness while writing this volume, I was always confident that Mom was
getting the best care possible. Sue, the "good daughter," did the heavy
lifting. I am forever grateful.

Contents

Grounded Theory

1

Introduction to Grounded Theory and Its Potential for Social Work

Grounded theory is one of the best known of the qualitative research methods, both within and outside of social work. However, almost 50 years after it was first described (Glaser & Strauss, 1967), it is still not always well understood. This volume aims to provide a clear, easy-to-understand description of grounded theory for beginning social work researchers and those who are new to grounded theory.

CHAPTER OVERVIEW

This chapter provides a basic introduction to grounded theory along with an invitation to the reader to learn about the method, its roots, and its development. I begin by arguing that grounded theory is of particular value for the social work profession. I introduce three excellent grounded theory studies that will be used throughout this pocket guide to illustrate the grounded theory method, and to show how it can be used in social work and related fields. I also provide some historical background on the method, emphasizing its common roots with those of the social work profession. I include an introduction to the theory of symbolic interactionism, because its ideas are central to both social work and grounded theory. Finally, I introduce the basic characteristics and key components of the grounded theory method and briefly discuss how it has evolved since the late 1960s, including recent developments such as constructivist and postmodern models. Several suggested exercises follow the chapter.

SOCIAL WORK AND THE PROMISE OF GROUNDED THEORY

Why should today's social work researchers learn about grounded theory, a qualitative method that was developed almost 50 years ago? Isn't it outdated and irrelevant to contemporary social work practice? Quite the contrary! The social work profession today needs to ensure that our services are of the highest quality. While much attention has focused on the measurement of the outcomes of our interventions, there is another equally important component of excellence that should be part of the debate. That is, both practice and research standards require that social work interventions and evaluations have a strong theoretical base. Quality social work services must be based in a solid understanding of human behavior and social environments. Likewise, research on interventions requires that we have theories that are applicable to practice situations. Many of the theories we use in our research and teach in master's in social work (MSW) programs come from the social sciences, not social work practice, and can be difficult to apply to practice situations. Some are too abstract, while others are problematic because they are based on models of human behavior that differ from the social work focus on "person in environment." While many social work practitioners develop conceptual models that are grounded in practice, sometimes called "practice wisdom," much of this theory never gets tested or disseminated. Social work researchers are taught a traditional (deductive) model of science that is based on theory testing. Without theory that fits the world of social work practice, we will never achieve our goal of developing and delivering quality social work services.

What does this all have to do with grounded theory? A great deal, actually. Grounded theory was designed to create theories that were empirically derived from real-world situations. The methodology grew from a view (in sociology) that because the grand theories developed by "armchair theorists" could not be empirically tested, a less abstract level of theory (called "middle range" theory) was needed. Because grounded theory creates theories that are derived directly from real-world settings, it has the potential to produce theories that can be used by social workers to guide practice. This theory can also be used to develop theoretically based interventions that can be tested in practice settings. In fact, when grounded theory was developed, the authors envisioned a collaborative venture between researchers and practitioners to test and adapt the theory in practice settings. Glaser and Strauss (1967) argued that theories developed using their model will be understandable by practitioners, and will "work" in real-world settings. (See Chapter 5 for further discussion of how this criterion is used to evaluate grounded theory.)

The fact that the methodology of grounded theory was designed to be of "use" is important for social worker researchers who aim to develop theories that can be applied in practice situations. Another reason that grounded theory is of particular value for social work is that both grounded theory and social work have common roots in symbolic inter-actionism, pragmatism, and the ideals of the Progressive Era. As a result, social work researchers find the assumptions and the procedures of grounded theory very comfortable. In emphasizing the common roots of social work and grounded theory, I do not mean to suggest that other qualitative traditions are not equally valuable to the profession. For example, Wells points out the value of narrative analysis to social work (2011). Before discussing this common background, I introduce three examples of grounded theory studies in social work, which illustrate the method and show how it can be used to inform social work practice.

INTRODUCTION TO EXEMPLAR GROUNDED THEORY STUDIES IN SOCIAL WORK

In this section, I provide a brief description of three social work grounded theory studies that I will use throughout the pocket guide to illustrate the grounded theory method.

Exemplar 1: Alaggia

Ramona Alaggia, who is on the Factor-Inwentash Faculty of Social Work at the University of Toronto, published an excellent grounded theory study on the ways mothers respond when they find out their young daughters have experienced sexual abuse by a family member (Alaggia, 2002). Her purpose was "to identify factors contributing to maternal response, and aspects of more and less supportive responses. . ." (p. 43). She started by comparing mothers who were supportive of their daughters and those who were not. Her study identified three broad categories of maternal response: *belief* (with a range from "unconditional belief" to "does not believe child"), *affective support,* and *behavioral support.* She also identified a "temporal dimension" of the maternal response. That is, some mothers' responses changed over time, while others' were more constant. Alaggia's grounded theory study revealed that maternal response is complex and multidimensional. Her study added the idea that maternal response varies over time. She discusses the implications of her results for social work clinicians, arguing that they could make mistakes if they don't recognize that mothers often change over time. Also, she emphasizes the importance of individualistic assessment and treatment, as well as self-examination on the part of the social worker concerning attitudes toward these mothers and the need to support them.

Exemplar #2: Anderson and Danis

A second exemplar study is by Kim Anderson and Fran Danis, from the School of Social Work at the University of Missouri-Columbia (Anderson & Danis, 2006).[1] They studied resistance and resilience in adult daughters of battered women. Their grounded theory project focused on the "strategies that girls used to overcome an oppressive home environment" (p. 419). They found that the daughters' strategies included "creating physical and mental escapes," "attempting to understand what was going on in the family," and "building support networks." They conclude that social workers ("helping professionals") should "help women recognize how their strategies of resistance led to their resilience" (p. 430). Their model emphasizes that strategies of resistance have been overlooked in previous research. They recommend that "resistance" be added to our notion of "resilience."

---

[1] Danis currently works at University of Texas, Arlington.

Exemplar #3: Yan

Miu Chung Yan's study of cultural tensions in cross-cultural social work practice also illustrates the grounded theory method (Yan, 2008a). In this study, Yan, from the School of Social Work, University of British Columbia, looked at "how social workers interact with their own cultures when they work with clients from a different culture" (p. 319). He found that minority social workers experience tensions when working with clients, not only because the clients come from cultures with values that differ or conflict with the dominant Western culture, but also because the social workers' own cultures conflict with the organizational (social work) values. A third type of conflict occurs when the organizational (social work) culture conflicts with the client's culture. This study identified several different types of cultural conflicts, greatly expanding the conceptualization of "cultural competence" in the field. Yan concludes that the social work profession needs to understand that cultural tensions in social work practice are multifaceted, and that previous models are inadequate. He emphasizes the importance of critical reflexivity in social workers, including an understanding of their own "socio-organizational position" (p. 327). He concludes, "Instead of focusing only on how individuals' cultures may affect the cause of the problem and the coping capability of the individuals, we should better articulate how other cultures, including those of our organizations and of the society at large, may influence our clients, as well as how various forms of cultural tension may affect our intervention process" (p. 327).

These studies show how grounded theory can contribute to social work, at both clinical and macro levels. Not only do they add to knowledge in an area that is important to practitioners, but also, moving beyond description, they develop theoretical models and show how practitioners (clinical or macro) can use them to improve practice.

THE COMMON ROOTS OF GROUNDED THEORY AND SOCIAL WORK

Although grounded theory was developed in sociology, it is very compatible with social work. This may be due to the common roots of the two fields, since grounded theory is based on symbolic interactionism, which, like social work, has roots in the Chicago of the Progressive Era. Social work and symbolic interactionism share many basic assumptions. (See discussion of symbolic interactionism below.)

Jane Addams, Hull House, and the University of Chicago

Chicago grew rapidly during the nineteenth century, from a small outpost to a major urban center. In 1890, it had over 300,000 residents, made up of migrants from rural areas as well as immigrants of Irish, German, Italian, Eastern European Jewish, and other backgrounds. Jane Addams, a founder of the social work profession in the United States, purchased an old home belonging to the Hull family in the heart of Chicago following a visit to Toynbee Hall in London (Deegan, 2005; Knight, 2010). There, she created a settlement house to help the immigrant families in the surrounding neighborhood.

Around the time Addams was developing Hull House, the Rockefeller family established the University of Chicago. Chicago soon became the center for the Progressive Movement, drawing idealists, creative thinkers, and activists from around the country. Addams and her colleagues at Hull House were central to this new social activism in Chicago. John Dewey came to Chicago from the University of Michigan to develop the departments of philosophy and psychology. George Herbert Mead, his friend and colleague at Michigan, soon followed. Dewey and Mead joined Jane Addams and her colleagues, the Abbotts, in their work on women's suffrage, labor conditions (including child labor), juvenile justice, and other causes. Dewey served on the board of Hull House. After Dewey left Chicago, Addams and Mead jointly planned and led the Garment Workers' Strike in 1910. Mead also served on the board of the University of Chicago Settlement House, and remained an active social reformer for many years (Cook, 1993).

In this period, activists and academics participated together in social action in the community as well as in researching, teaching and writing at the university. At the time, there was no clear division between academia and social action. Dewey and Mead (as well as other faculty members at the University of Chicago) worked with Addams in the Hull House kitchen, planning strategy and discussing theory (Deegan, 2005). While advocating for and building services for the poor, Addams and her colleagues also conducted research on the causes of poverty and crime, such as *Hull House Papers and Maps* (1895). Addams's research on the neighborhoods surrounding Hull House influenced what would later develop into the research methods of the Chicago School (urban ethnography). Mead, too, worked on the development of a "social survey" for Chicago, based on the model of the Pittsburgh survey (Cook, 1993; Zimbalist 1977). The development of social science theory was also a central part of their work for social justice. Addams published articles periodically in the new sociology journal based at the University of Chicago, *The American Journal of Sociology* (Deegan, 2005). Mead's theory, later labeled "symbolic interactionism," was developed out of this interaction of social action, research, and theory development.

The social work profession in the United States was strongly influenced by this fusion of social action, research, and social theory. In 1905, the Chicago School of Civics and Philanthropy, the first school of social work in the United States, was established by Breckenridge and Abbott, a colleague of Addams at Hull House. Both Dewey and Mead lectured at this new social work school in its early days. The fledgling social work profession used Dewey's educational model, which emphasized learning by doing, placing a heavy emphasis on field education. In 1920, this school was incorporated into the University of Chicago and renamed the School of Social Service Administration (SSSA). The model of social work education developed at the SSSA had a formative influence on the development of the social work profession. Over time, the SSSA and the academic departments of the university grew apart, although both the social work profession and the Chicago School continued to reflect the joint work of their founders. (For further information on the Chicago School of Sociology, see Bulmer, 1984.)

Pragmatism, Symbolic Interactionism, and Social Work Practice and Research

In this section, I provide a brief introduction to pragmatism and symbolic interactionism, because the grounded theory method was based in these theoretical models. While it may seem like a digression, I feel strongly that any researcher who is exploring grounded theory needs to have a basic understanding of these theories at a minimum. (The reasons for this will become clear in the later sections of this chapter, as well as in Chapters 3 and 4.)

Pragmatism was central to both social work and the philosophy of the University of Chicago Department of Sociology. This philosophy, developed by Pierce and Dewey, emphasized doing what works, instead of adhering uncritically to theoretical or philosophical principles (Locke, 2007; Strubing, 2007). "Pragmatism is a philosophical movement that . . . claims[s] that an ideology or proposition is true if it works satisfactorily, that the meaning of a proposition is to be found in the practical consequences of accepting it, and that unpractical ideas are to be rejected" (McDermid, 2006). A current social work text defines it as follows: "reality does not exist independent of meanings that are created, defined and acted upon by people according to their usefulness" (Robbins, Chatterjee, & Canda, 2006, p. 321). As a practice profession, social work often takes a pragmatic view, although it may not always be acknowledged.

I now turn to an introduction of symbolic interactionist theory. Mead integrated ideas developed by other sociologists of the time, such as Dewey, James, Thomas, Znaniecki, and Cooley, into a single theory (Blumer, 1969; Morris, 1967; Strauss, 1977). As discussed above, Mead's ideas were formulated as he worked with Dewey and Addams to improve the lives of Chicago's needy populations. Through these experiences, he saw people actively interacting with and shaping their environments. Mead thought that other ideas prominent at the time viewed human beings as reactive rather than active. In his essays and classes, he argued against psychodynamic, behavioral, and sociological models that portrayed human beings as shaped by internal drives, external rewards and punishments, or macro social forces (Blumer, 1969; Mead, 1934; Strauss & Mead 1956). In contrast, Mead viewed human beings as taking actions that are based on meanings shaped through social interactions.

Mead taught at the University of Chicago over a period of many years, where he developed and disseminated his ideas through his teaching and in a series of essays. However, he never consolidated his ideas into a single theory. After his death in 1931, his students wrote *Mind, Self and Society* (Mead, 1934) based on their class notes. In 1969 (almost 40 years after Mead's death), one of Mead's ex-students, Herbert Blumer, consolidated and expanded Mead's theory, coining the term "symbolic interaction" (Blumer, 1969). Box 1.1 provides a list of the basic concepts

---

Box 1.1 Basic Concepts of Symbolic Interaction Theory

- The act
- Significant symbols
- Interpretation
- Meaning
- The mind
- The "self"
- The "generalized other"
- Social interaction
- Shared meaning
- Process (social process)
- Society

(Source: Ritzer, 2010a.)

Box 1.2 Basic Tenets of Symbolic Interactionism

- "Human beings act toward things on the basis of the meanings that the things have for them."
- "The meaning of such things is derived from, or arises out of, the social interaction that one has with one's fellows."
- "These meanings are handled in, and modified through, an interpretive process used by the person in dealing with the things that he encounters."

(Source: Blumer, 1969, p. 2.)

---

that are used in symbolic interaction theory (Ritzer, 2010a, 2010b). Box 1.2 lists the basic tenants of symbolic interactionism.

In a recent social work text, symbolic interaction is defined as follows:

> The dynamic process of interaction between the person and the environment that results in a self that is continually growing and changing. Symbolic interaction is based on the premise that identity involves shared significant symbols (or shared meanings) that emerge in the process of interaction with others. (Robbins et al., 2006, p. 296)

It is also important to understand that in symbolic interactionism, the nature of reality is dynamic, not static. The "self" constantly changes as the individual interprets meanings through social interactions, takes actions, and evaluates the consequences. Also, symbolic interaction theory emphasizes social process.

Blumer's volume on symbolic interactionism (1969) played an important role in the development of grounded theory, because not only did it make Mead's ideas more accessible, but it also discussed the type of research methodology that would be needed to study symbolic interactionist concepts. Blumer advocated for qualitative methodology, based on observation and interviews, because this was the only way to study a dynamic reality that was based on the interpretation of meanings, social interactions, and identity (Blumer, 1969). (For a detailed discussion of the development of the ideas and methods of the Chicago School of Sociology, see Gilgun, 1999, 2007.)

The social work profession and symbolic interaction theory share many common perspectives. Symbolic interaction theory focuses on the interaction between the individual and the environment, while social work practice traditionally focuses on the "person in environment" (Greene & Ephross, 1991). Both view individuals as active beings who develop their identity based on interactions with individuals in their social networks and on meanings derived from the larger society. Social work's focus on empowerment reflects the view of individuals as active participants who shape their environments, and not as passive recipients of services. The importance of the self in symbolic interactionism and the importance of the "use of self" in clinical social work illustrate the common perspective of the two fields. (See Forte, 2004, for a more extensive discussion of symbolic interactionism and social work.)

Since grounded theory is the qualitative methodology that grew out of symbolic interactionism, it is not surprising that grounded theory methods have clear parallels to social work practice. Gilgun has identified a number of these similarities, calling the correspondence between social work practice in clinical settings and grounded theory "hand into glove" (Gilgun, 1994). Of course, there are also clear differences, as one is a practice method and the other a research method (Padgett, 1998). But this is yet another connection between social work and grounded theory that stems from their common roots.

Origins of Grounded Theory

The link between pragmatism and symbolic interactionism was provided by Anselm Strauss, who completed his PhD at the University of Chicago, where he studied with Blumer. He had a strong background in symbolic interaction theory and in the Chicago "field study" method. Strauss began his academic career in the Midwest, but was recruited to San Francisco by the School of Nursing at the University of California at San Francisco (UCSF) to develop a new doctoral program (Stern, 2009; Stern & Porr, 2011). At the time, Glaser had just come back to California after obtaining his PhD at Columbia University. There, Glaser had been trained in quantitative research methods, under Merton and Lazarsfeld. Glaser and Strauss met in San Francisco, and Strauss invited Glaser to work on his research project on dying. The grounded theory method that they developed reflected a combination of Strauss's background in symbolic interactionism and qualitative methods and Glaser's interest in developing theory and training in quantitative research methods.

The term "grounded theory" originated in 1967 with the publication of *The Discovery of Grounded Theory* (Glaser & Strauss, 1967). They had recently completed a four-year study of dying in San Francisco hospitals (Glaser & Strauss, 1965, 1968). In *Discovery*, they described the research process they used in this study and advocated for a wider application of their approach, which they labeled "grounded theory." Much of the methodology in this classic volume was not really new, but was descriptive of methods that had been taught at the Chicago School for many years.

There were, however, some important differences. First, Glaser and Strauss identified the aim of grounded theory as the development of "middle-range theory" (1967). This focus on theory development is the major characteristic that distinguishes grounded theory from other qualitative methods. In *Discovery*, Glaser and Strauss criticized the traditional Chicago-style urban ethnographies because they provided detailed descriptions but did not generate theories that would be useful for practice. They also criticized the type of "logico-deductive" theory that was popular at the time (1967) because it was based primarily on speculation and deduction, and was not empirically based. In doing so, they joined a debate that was current in sociology at that time. Postwar sociology had been greatly impacted by the technological developments that made quantitative research possible, such as advances in statistics and the use of computers, leading to the development of the field of survey research. Researchers began to generate extensive amounts of quantitative data, which were immediately attacked for being "a-theoretical." Robert K. Merton (who was one of Glaser's instructors at Columbia) argued in response that sociology needed "theories of the middle range" (Merton, 1968). In *Discovery*, Strauss and Glaser agreed with Merton that much of sociological theory, which they called "Grand Theory," was too broad to apply to "real world" situations. They argued for a new way to develop theory where theory would be based on empirical observation. The resulting "grounded theories" would be "middle range" theories, applicable to real-world situations.

Second, while the Chicago tradition had been to send students out into the field with little methodological instruction, Glaser and Strauss provided a detailed description of how the research should be conducted and evaluated. This was a major advance that facilitated the adoption of the method across the country and around the world. The codification of the method in the *Discovery* book is attributed to Glaser, and his training at Columbia (with Merton) accounts for the focus on the need to develop "middle-range theories."

Grounded theory combined traditions in sociology, as discussed above. It also combined a social science (sociology) and a health profession (nursing). The courses and seminars that Glaser and Strauss developed were offered to PhD students in both nursing and sociology. Their research was focused in practice settings. As a practice profession, the fact that the grounded theory method developed out of an interaction between theory and practice is of special importance for social work.

CHARACTERISTICS OF GROUNDED THEORY

I turn now to a basic description of grounded theory, including its goals, the key components, the logic used in theory building, and the process of doing grounded theory (see Box 1.3). In a recent volume on grounded theory by the students of Glaser and Strauss, Morse writes, "Grounded theory is not a prescribed method that uses a particular 'level of data' and formulistic techniques to calculate a solution. . . . Grounded theory is a way of thinking about data–processes of conceptualization–of theorizing from data, so that the end result is a theory that the scientist produces from data collected by interviewing and observing everyday life" (Morse et al., 2009, p. 18). In grounded theory research, data gathering and data analysis are simultaneous.

Box 1.3 Characteristics of Grounded Theory

- Goal of theory development
- Based on symbolic interaction concepts
- Multistage process with cycles of data gathering and data analysis, using abductive logic
- Includes key components of:
  - Theoretical sensitivity
  - Constant comparison
  - Theoretical sampling
  - Theoretical saturation

The Goal of Grounded Theory: Theory Development

To truly understand grounded theory, it is important to recognize the importance of the word "theory." Theory is central, used not only in the name of the method but also in many of the key terms used in grounded theory, all of which emphasize that the purpose of the methodology is theory development (see section below). This focus on the development of middle-range theory is the primary way that grounded theory differs from other qualitative methods (Corbin & Strauss, 2008; Hood, 2007. Although qualitative studies done in other traditions may have theoretical implications, their aim is more likely to be a detailed ("thick") description of a culture or a setting (ethnography) or of the "meanings" individuals ascribe to aspects of their cultures or their lives (phenomenology). Narrative studies aim to describe and analyze the respondents' "story" (Wells, 2011). In contrast to these models, the primary goal of grounded theory studies is to build theory.

Key Components of Grounded Theory

The key components of grounded theory that were described in *Discovery* (1967) are constant comparison, theoretical sensitivity, theoretical sampling, and theoretical saturation. Each of these components is briefly introduced here and taken up in more detail in the following chapters. While it is important to understand the meaning of the individual components, in the grounded theory method these components are used in combination to develop theory from data. (This broader process is

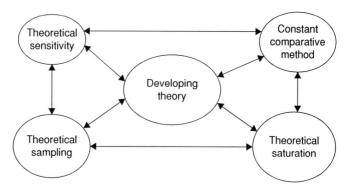

Figure 1.1 Key components of grounded theory.

described in the next section). Figure 1.1 shows the interaction among the key components.

Theoretical Sensitivity

Theoretical sensitivity is the ability of the researcher to be analytic, that is, to see what is being studied in theoretical terms and to go beyond the entities themselves and to identify characteristics of these entities. Theoretical sensitivity is based on familiarity with sociological theories and concepts, but it is also based on personal experience, professional experience, and temperament. Theoretical sensitivity is something that grows over time and is related to "many years of thinking theoretically" (Glaser & Strauss, 1967, p. 46).

Constant Comparison

Constant comparison is the basic method used in grounded theory to create theory out of empirical data. By comparing case to case (whether this be individual cases or cases based on organizations or larger structures, such as societies), the researcher develops "concepts." The process of constant comparison makes similarities and differences among cases apparent. Conceptual categories are specified and described, based on the data.

Theoretical Sampling

Sampling in grounded theory is driven by the developing theory. Since the theory evolves as the study progresses, the sampling strategy changes over the course of the study. Therefore, it is not determined in advance.

In grounded theory, the goal is to develop a theory that is useful in situations similar to the one in which the theory was generated. That is, the theory should work in similar situations. The sample used to generate the theory is not "representative" in the same way that it is in a quantitative study. In quantitative research, the characteristics of the sample focused on are often demographic. In a grounded theory study, however, demographic characteristics may be irrelevant to the theory. The aim instead is a sample that allows thorough exploration of the relevant concepts. Since this cannot be determined in advance, a sampling strategy should not be predetermined because the theory could be restricted by a sampling strategy that turns out to be irrelevant to the emerging theory.

Theoretical Saturation

Theoretical saturation means "no additional data are being found whereby the sociologist can develop properties of the category" (Glaser & Strauss, 1967, p. 61). The research continues until the researcher reaches a point of "saturation." That is, no new concepts are emerging, and the theory is supported by the data. Glaser and Strauss indicate that not all categories and concepts need to be developed to a point of saturation, but saturation is essential for what they call "core categories" (1967). (See further discussion in Chapter 4.)

The Logic of Grounded Theory

Because grounded theory focuses on the generation of theory that is grounded in data, it begins with immersion in data, using inductive logic. That is, it begins with data collection and generates theory out of that data. The process does not end there, however, since grounded theory is a multistage process. The researcher begins by using inductive logic, but the developing theory is then explored, expanded, and tested as the researcher returns to the field. This step of testing the theory by gathering additional data uses deductive (theory-testing) logic. Because grounded theory uses both inductive and deductive logic in a "back and forth" process of theory generation (inductive) and theory testing (deductive), the logic of grounded theory is "abductive" (Locke, 2007; Reichertz, 2007; Richardson & Kramer, 2006). Figure 1.2 provides an illustration of this process.

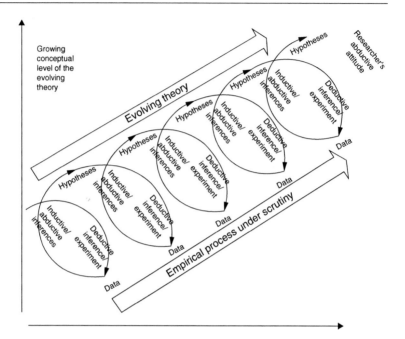

Figure 1.2 The grounded theory process. Source: Strubing (2007, p. 595).

The Grounded Theory Process

The components work together in a multistage process that builds theory. The researcher first selects a topic and begins to gather some data, using his or her **theoretical sensitivity**. Then, he or she uses **constant comparison** to generate concepts from the data, while applying **theoretical sensitivity** to understand the concepts and raise them to a higher conceptual level. **Theoretical sampling** is used to guide the next stage of data gathering and to further develop and verify the concepts. This process, called the grounded theory method (GTM), continues in multiple stages until **theoretical saturation** is reached (see Figure 1.1).

Unfortunately, there are many studies in the social work literature that describe themselves as "grounded theory" but that lack most of the characteristics of grounded theory discussed here (O'Connor, Netting, & Thomas, 2008) (see exercise #3). It is not uncommon for researchers (in social work as well as many other fields) to borrow some of the procedures (e.g., open coding) used in grounded theory and then use the term "grounded theory" to describe their study. Studies that use some grounded theory techniques but that do not use the process described above to generate theory are not true grounded theory studies. (See discussion of levels of grounded theory studies in Chapter 6.)

EVOLUTION OF GROUNDED THEORY SINCE 1967

Grounded theory's popularity increased steadily after *Discovery* was published in 1967. When students and researchers tried to apply the grounded theory method using only the information in *Discovery*, without the support of the type of graduate seminar offered at UCSF, they often ran into problems. Many got stuck or overwhelmed or were simply unsure how and when to apply the various components of the method. In response to this need, both Glaser (1978) and Strauss (1987) wrote texts to further explain and clarify the grounded theory method. In his text, Strauss presented one of his UCSF seminars verbatim (Strauss, 1987). These books were only partly successful in meeting the needs of new grounded theory researchers. Few professors were able to duplicate Strauss's seminars in their classrooms. The elaborate scheme of "coding families" that Glaser developed (Glaser, 1978) was helpful for some but confusing for others. These texts also revealed differences between Glaser and Strauss that had not been apparent when they worked together. Glaser and Strauss came to have different ideas about grounded theory and how it should be practiced. These differences probably reflect their very different backgrounds and can be viewed as reflective of different epistemological assumptions. Glaser left UCSF to found and direct The Grounded Theory Institute, which teaches and disseminates his version of grounded theory. As a result of their differences, two styles or models of grounded theory emerged (Annells, 1996; Melia, 1996; Stern & Porr 2011). Glaser's later work emphasized the positivist assumptions of grounded theory, while Strauss emphasized its more constructivist (interactionist) aspects. (See discussion below on epistemological challenges to grounded theory.)

In 1990, Strauss published *Basics of Qualitative Research*, with Juliet Corbin, then his postgraduate student. *Basics* was written as an introductory text that greatly simplified the grounded theory method. It included descriptions of specific techniques, illustrations, exercises, and answers to questions that reflect the problems researchers (especially students) encounter when they try to conduct grounded theory studies. Second and third editions of this text were published after Strauss's death in 1996 (Strauss & Corbin, 1998; Corbin & Strauss, 2008). The differences between Glaser and Strauss concerning the practice of grounded theory became even clearer when Glaser published a volume that was highly critical of the *Basics* text (Glaser, 1992).

Despite these differences, both Glaser and Strauss trained many students at UCSF in nursing and sociology in the grounded theory method. It is these students who are now the leading grounded theory researchers and who make up the ranks of the grounded theory professorate. (Morse et al., 2009). Through their books, training workshops, and now the Internet, their training is not limited to UCSF, as the method has been widely disseminated throughout the world.

The Epistemological Challenge to Grounded Theory

The later evolution of grounded theory came about largely in response to changes that were taking place in universities and in the broader field of qualitative research. The assumptions of quantitative research continued to be challenged while qualitative research gained legitimacy. In social work, this conflict took the form of the "paradigm wars" (Hartman, 1990), as newer worldviews questioned many of the assumptions of positivist science. In the late twentieth century, various authors developed classifications for different types of research. For example, Denzin placed all quantitative research in the positivist or postpositivist epistemological camp, while qualitative research was seen to be rooted in constructivist, postmodern, or critical philosophies. Others labeled the grounded theory method "positivist" or "postpositivist" based on some of the language used in *Discovery*. This classification is based on statements that appear to be based on an assumption that there is a reality that can be known and that the researcher can be an objective observer. For example, the idea that theory is "discovered" suggests that a reality exists outside of the researcher. The idea that theory "emerges" from the data is based on a concept of the researcher as an objective outsider to the process. The theory that results is described as a tool to "explain and predict," a common goal of positivist science. In fact, these issues were not discussed in any of the "classic" volumes on grounded theory, since grounded theory was developed before the epistemological debates. Not until the third edition of *Basics* was the question of epistemology taken up explicitly by Corbin (Corbin & Strauss, 2008), without coming down strongly on either side.

Grounded theory researchers have reacted to the challenges, as well as the changing times, in different ways. Glaser has stayed closest to the original perspective, arguing that what is "discovered" in grounded theory is "real." This model is sometimes labeled "positivist." In this model, the theory that is produced is seen as something that can be tested ("verified") with traditional quantitative methods. Charmaz (one of Glaser and Strauss's students) argues that grounded theory methods are compatible with a constructivist philosophy (2006, 2011). In a constructivist view, the theory produced is seen as a co-construction between researcher and respondents, dependent on time, place, and circumstance. In this version, the theory is based on interactions between the researcher and the data. The researcher "constructs" the theory, or "co-constructs" it in collaboration with the study participants and/or others (Rodwell, 1998). In "constructivist" grounded theory, grounded theory procedures that are based on the assumption of single reality are omitted. More recently, "situational analysis," a postmodern version of grounded theory, was developed by Adele Clarke (Clarke, 2005; Clarke & Frieze, 2007). Clarke is a sociologist of science who studied at UCSF with Glaser and Strauss. As a result of these developments, there are now a range of grounded theory models based on varied epistemological assumptions.

Figure 1.3 provides a comparison of three "ideal type" models of grounded theory—a positivist model, a constructivist model, and a pragmatic model. I present this figure with some trepidation because it oversimplifies the issues, and there is a danger that it will be applied in a rigid way. This would be a mistake. Rather, it should be used by students who find this type of device helpful to understand some of the debates in the grounded theory literature. The positivist model is associated with Glaser. Charmaz advocates for a constructivist version of grounded theory.

Personally, I do not think that grounded theory can be fit easily into any single framework, nor are the different versions (positivist, postpositivist, classic, constructivist, postmodern) as clearly differentiated from

	Ontology	Epistemology	Methodology
Positivist	Assumes that reality exists and can be discovered	Theory is discovered by the researcher	No literature review is done until after the data analysis
		Theory emerges from the data when grounded theory procedures are used	A "core category" emerges from the analysis
		The researcher aims to enter the field as a "tabla rosa" (blank slate)	All other categories are related to the "core category"
		Researcher maintains objectivity and minimizes bias	Researcher is erased from the write-up of the analysis
Constructivist	All reality is constructed	The constructed perspectives of the researcher and the respondents are equally valuable	The researcher and his/her perspective is a central component of the study
	There are multiple realities	The researcher cannot be separated from the study	The researcher uses reflexivity to make his/her constructions visible
	Relativist		Multiple perspectives are presented
			The components of the single "core category" and a "basic social process" are omitted in the analysis
Pragmatist	Accepts external reality	Can incorporate both objectivist and subjectivist points of view	Can use methods from both positivist and constructivist grounded theory models
	Chooses assumptions about reality that are most useful for the study's purpose	Chooses the stance for the researcher that is most useful for the study's purpose	Chooses methods that are most useful for the study's purpose

Figure 1.3 Epistemologies of grounded theory (based on Tashakkori & Teddlie, 1998).

each other as they are sometimes presented. One reason why grounded theory is so valuable is because it is a kind of hybrid. As described above, grounded theory was born out of the work of a quantitative (positivist) researcher (Glaser) and a qualitative researcher trained in symbolic interaction theory (Strauss). Both men's views changed as they worked together and learned from each other (Stern & Porr, 2011). When I examine *Discovery* (Glaser & Strauss, 1967), for each statement I find that suggests that there is a single, knowable reality, I can find another that suggests a complex, ever-changing, constructed view of reality. For each reference to the objective researcher, I can find another that shows that the authors recognized that true objectivity is impossible to achieve. Trying to make grounded theory "fit" a single model risks losing the unique character of this method. Instead, I support an "agnostic" position that blends the most useful features of the different models depending on the needs of each study.

For this reason, I have added a pragmatist model to Figure 1.3. Pragmatism is highly compatible with the intellectual origins of grounded theory (Kelle, 2007; Star, 2007; Strubing, 2007) and with social work. Adopting a pragmatic framework means that one does not have to choose one side or the other but can use whatever model and techniques are most useful for a specific research project. The researcher can choose to act "as if" there is a reality when it is useful to do so (Tashakkori & Teddlie, 1998). A pragmatic model is often a good option for social work researchers, who tend to be more interested in the project itself than in some of the broader philosophical debates (Padgett, 2004, 2008). In my opinion, Hartman's position on "Many Ways of Knowing" holds up today (Hartman, 1990). We need all kinds of knowledge, and endless debates on which method is "best" are not usually productive. In some cases, a positivist (or postpositivist) perspective may be helpful to the profession from a pragmatic perspective, as when examining the effectiveness of interventions. As a practice field, responsible to our clients, our communities, and our colleagues, an epistemological stand that does not allow the existence of a "reality" may not be considered compatible with our professional responsibilities. Similarly, the view that researchers cannot be objective may be attractive, but incompatible with the worldview of potential funders or government bodies (and third-party payers). Fortunately, grounded theory can be used with different assumptions, depending on the circumstance.

CHAPTER SUMMARY

In this chapter, I have argued that social workers should explore grounded theory research. While grounded theory is not new, I do not feel it has fully reached its potential in social work. This is because it has often been misunderstood, and many so-called grounded theory studies never actually develop theory. Theory development is a primary reason why it has enormous potential for social work. We need the type of "middle range," empirically based theory that grounded theory can provide. While some have argued that we do not need theory (Thyer, 1994, 2001), I think this is because the theories that are most used in the field are often not very helpful in a practice situation. In contrast, theory that is drawn directly from practice situations would be enormously valuable to practitioners. As we try to develop interventions that are theoretically based, we need theories that are directly applicable to practice situations. I think that grounded theory holds the promise of just this type of theory. Like the children's story Goldilocks, theories developed with the grounded theory method are not too abstract, and not too concrete, but "just right."

Compared with other models of qualitative research, social workers will find grounded theory very familiar. Like social work, it focuses best when used with a problem that focuses on the "person in environment." Social workers are already comfortable with the language of symbolic interactionism, on which grounded theory is based. Also, the fact that grounded theory is based in pragmatism is also a good fit with the social work profession. It is my hope that this pocket guide will stimulate social work researchers to realize the potential of this method.

Long before I began to explore qualitative approaches in my own research, I came across a grounded theory study, which had a profound impact on me. Shortly before receiving my PhD degree, I was diagnosed with a chronic illness. Years later, I came across a book by Anselm Strauss and colleagues, which contained a chapter by one of Strauss's students, Carolyn Wiener (Wiener, 1984). While I did not realize it at that time, this was a grounded theory study of my own disease. When I read the chapter, I literally *gasped* with recognition! What was being described was true to my experience. The research described what my life was like on a day-to-day basis—what the challenges were "balancing the hope and the dread"—and strategies I used like "covering up," "keeping up," and "pacing." These were all things I did but had never discussed with anyone else, and had certainly never hoped to find described in a research study! Another aspect of this grounded theory study that I loved was that the "respondents" (e.g., "patients") were listened to, their perspective was valued, and, probably most important to me, they were presented as active problem solvers instead of as the passive recipients of services I experienced in the medical setting. While it was not until many years later that I shifted my focus (both research and teaching) from quantitative to qualitative methods, I think it was the recognition that Wiener had captured the essence of my experience that ultimately led to my desire to learn about and to practice grounded theory research.

I love doing grounded theory research, and it is my goal to share this love with other social work researchers. Grounded theory is positioned between the hurly burly of the practice world and the more abstract world of ideas. Grounded theory allows you to think creatively, at an abstract level, but it also requires you to return to the real world and adapt your theory to better fit the world of practice. Developing ideas is stimulating and fun (although hard!), and seeing how they can be used to improve practice can be extremely gratifying. Jane Addams, who combined social activism with research and theory, once said, "It is ideas which mold the lives of men [sic]" (Knight, 2010, p. 140). What could be better than to dance freely between ideas and practice?

SUGGESTED EXERCISES

1. Read each of the exemplar social work grounded theory studies. Consider how the middle-range theories developed in each can be used in social work practice or education.
2. Consider a research topic that interests you. Try to use terms and assumptions from symbolic interaction theory to describe the topic. Can you identify human "actors"? Actions? Interactions? Roles? Can you describe the topic in terms of a "self" that is shaped by interactions between the individual and his or her social world?
3. For each of the exemplar social work grounded theory studies, identify the key components of grounded theory in the articles.

Compare these studies to a qualitative study in your field of interest. How do they differ?

4. Find an article in your field of interest that uses the term "grounded theory" to describe its methodology. Consider which of the key components of the grounded theory method were used by the authors. Do you think the term "grounded theory" accurately describes the study methodology?

2

Getting Started

In Chapter 1, I provided an overview of grounded theory, including its history, its basis in symbolic interaction theory, and the value of this method for social work today. In this chapter, I focus on how to decide whether grounded theory is an appropriate research strategy for your study. I begin with a brief discussion of when qualitative methods such as grounded theory are most helpful. I then describe in more depth the basic characteristics and key components of grounded theory that were introduced in the last chapter. I discuss how each of them can be used in the consideration of when to use grounded theory, and how the various characteristics of grounded theory impact problem formulation and study design. The three exemplar grounded theory studies in social work are used to illustrate these characteristics and key components. Finally, I discuss the development of a research proposal in grounded theory research.

Determining if Your Research Is Appropriate for Qualitative Research

If a research question is not a good fit with qualitative research, it will not be a good idea for a grounded theory study, since grounded theory is in the qualitative research family. Grounded theory and other qualitative traditions share many common characteristics. Therefore, the first step in deciding whether to use grounded theory is to make sure that the study is appropriate for qualitative research methods. When my students propose research questions that are not good candidates for grounded theory, it is often not because of something specific to grounded theory itself, but simply because the proposed question is not a good fit for qualitative research. There are many excellent resources on qualitative research that clarify the types of research questions that are appropriate to these methods (Creswell, 2007; Maxwell, 2005; Padgett, 2008). I will begin with a brief summary of a couple of them.

Box 2.1 contains a list of conditions when a qualitative methodology is an appropriate choice, based on Padgett (2008). (I have added a seventh reason to Padgett's list.)

Figure 2.1 illustrates a research topic where a qualitative methodology may have been more suitable than a quantitative survey methodology.

Maxwell distinguishes between process and variance questions (Maxwell, 2005), arguing that qualitative research is particularly good at dealing with "process" questions. These are questions that explore how a social process works rather than questions that attempt to determine causality. Research questions that focus on explaining variance, rather than exploring process, may not be good candidates for a qualitative study. If your research question is about the variance explained in one variable by a second variable, you do not have a process question (Maxwell, 2005). While the question of the ability of qualitative methods to explore causal questions is controversial (see discussion in Miles & Huberman, 1994), I find Maxwell's distinction between process and variance questions very helpful. Students who have been trained in quantitative methods often generate variance questions at first when they are doing qualitative projects. Before you can decide which qualitative method to use, you need to learn to generate an appropriate qualitative research question.

Box 2.1 Appropriate Goals for Qualitative Research

1. Topic about which little is known
2. Topic of sensitivity and emotional depth
3. Studies of the "lived experience" from the perspectives of those who live it and create meaning from it
4. Studies to understand the "black box" of practice, programs, and interventions
5. Studies to understand unexpected quantitative findings
6. Studies that combine advocacy with research
   (Padgett, 2008, pp. 15–16)
7. Studies of complex social processes

"*Next question: I believe that life is a constant striving for balance, requiring frequent tradeoffs between morality and necessity, within a cyclic pattern of joy and sadness, forging a trail of bittersweet memories until one slips, inevitably, into the jaws of death. Agree or disagree?*"

Figure 2.1 "Next question." Source: © George Price/The New Yorker Collection/ www.cartoonbank.com

Although there is strong interest today in intervention research, doing qualitative research (including grounded theory) is not an appropriate way to determine whether or not a particular intervention "works."

This is a variance question. Good qualitative questions in the field of evidence-based practice might describe the process of the intervention, the experience of individuals receiving the intervention, the experience of the workers providing the intervention, strategies used by clients or workers when an intervention is introduced, or conditions when agencies are or are not receptive to pressures to adopt new ways of practicing. Qualitative studies might also explore how practitioners think about agency initiatives to encourage use of evidence- based interventions, or strategies they use to avoid using them. In Padgett's terms, a qualitative study might productively look into the "black box" of the intervention (#4 in Box 2.1), or a quantitative researcher who learned through a randomized controlled trial (RCT) that an intervention didn't work as expected might use a qualitative strategy to explore why not (#5 in Box 2.1).

Assessing Potential Bias

Once you have an appropriate qualitative question, you need to consider whether this is a good project for you. Some qualitative projects ask good questions but may not be a good fit for a particular researcher because of potential "researcher bias" (Padgett, 2008). Likely sources of bias need to be considered when judging any potential qualitative research project, whether or not it is grounded theory. In all qualitative projects, it is important to be able to see the world from the respondents' perspective. Researchers need to think about their backgrounds and how they may both help and hinder the proposed study. When you have personal life experience or professional experience in the area of your topic, you are more likely to be able to understand the experience of your informants. However, it is possible to be too close to the topic (see Padgett, 2008, pp. 20–21) and be unable to see beyond your own experience. For example, if a researcher has strong views on the topic or if the study has the potential to stir up painful past experiences for the researcher, the researcher's focus may shift away from the respondent. (This issue is discussed further in the section on "theoretical sensitivity.")

Qualitative researchers also need to consider the possibility of "respondent bias" for a proposed study (Padgett, 2008). An example would be when a researcher is studying a program that has a strong ideology or worldview that is not open to interpretation, such as the

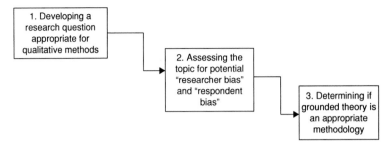

Figure 2.2 Selecting an appropriate methodology.

Alcoholics Anonymous (AA) programs. It may be difficult for the researcher to gain access to the social process because the program itself presents a specific interpretation of their own experience to the participants (e.g., in the AA example, "This is what is happening to you because you are in Step One"). When doing interviews, the researcher is likely to hear that interpretation from people who are participating in the program. (See Chapter 5 for further discussion of the issue of "respondent and researcher bias.") Figure 2.2 illustrates these early steps in selecting a grounded theory methodology.

DETERMINING IF YOUR RESEARCH PROJECT IS APPROPRIATE FOR GROUNDED THEORY

Once you have an appropriate qualitative research question and a topic that is relatively free from researcher and respondent bias, you are ready to consider whether or not grounded theory is a good fit for your project. As discussed in the previous chapter, grounded theory has a distinct history, purpose, and set of methods. Some study topics and methods fit better with grounded theory than others. In this section, I illustrate how the central characteristics of grounded theory can help you determine if grounded theory is a good choice or if another qualitative method might better suit your particular study (see Box 2.2).

I will review each of these characteristics, discuss how they impact the choice of grounded theory methodology, and illustrate using the three exemplar social work grounded theory studies.

Box 2.2 Selection of a Grounded Theory Design

- Is your goal to develop theory?
- Does your problem fit with symbolic interactionist assumptions and level of analysis?
- Can you implement a multistage process using the key components of grounded theory?
  - Will you have access to your population over time?
  - Do you have access to a population with a wide variety of characteristics?
  - Do you have a time table that allows you to reach theoretical saturation?
- Do you have a temperament that is compatible with the grounded theory model?

Goal of Theory Development

As discussed in Chapter 1, the goal of grounded theory studies is to develop "middle-range theory." In social work, appropriate areas are those of relevance to the profession where little theory has been developed or where existing theory is too abstract to be of practical use to social workers. For example, populations or problem areas that are new to social work are often very appropriate for grounded theory studies. If your aim is not to develop a theory, other models of qualitative research might be better suited to your study. For example, if your goal is to describe a culture, a community, or a large, complex system, ethnography might be better suited to your need. If your goal is to tell a respondent's story or to go deeply into the meaning-making process of a lived experience, then narrative or phenomenological techniques might be a better fit. I'm exaggerating the distinction between these methods for instructional purposes. In fact, the differences are often somewhat blurry.

Because the aim of grounded theory research is to develop a theory, a study in a field where there is a strong theoretical consensus may not be conducive to grounded theory methodology. In social work, there are many fields where there is already well-developed theory and a good case cannot be made for a study whose aim is to develop theory. Sometimes researchers may initially think that they want to develop theory, but as they work on the project, it is clear that they cannot get outside of the existing theoretical model in the field. If your study topic is in the field of mental illness, for example, and you have been trained in a diagnostic framework, your grounded theory study may simply re-create the existing diagnostic framework. (The diagnostic framework also presents problems because it is based in a medical model of human behavior. See discussion below on symbolic interactionism.)

Each of the three exemplar grounded theory studies had a goal of theory development.

Exemplar #1: In her study on maternal support in child sexual abuse (2002), Alaggia justified her use of grounded theory methodology on the basis of a lack of theory in the area of maternal support in child sexual abuse. She argued that the child sexual abuse literature showed a lack of clarity and preciseness of the concept of maternal support. In addition, the few measures of maternal support that exist were not built on a solid theoretical understanding. "A qualitative approach such as grounded theory method accommodates non-linear associations and dynamics involved in complex situations like intra-familial child sexual abuse. Additionally, grounded theory moves beyond description of the experiences under investigation to developing a theory that explains the phenomenon studied [author provides citations]" (p. 43).

Exemplar #2: Anderson and Danis's (2006) study of adult daughters of battered women also had a goal of theory development. The authors point out that "previous research and theory building have been insufficient in specifying hypotheses for testing resilience" (p. 420). . . . "A theory of resilience or a description of meaningful constructs is lacking that may be used to integrate the various studies of risk and protective factors into a coherent whole" (p. 421). They critique research on resilience for failing to identify "strategies of resistance to childhood oppression that lead to resilience" (p. 421). Their goal was to develop theory, because they argue that not all concepts in this area have been identified. They also show how theory can lead to improvement of social work practice. "Because little is known in this area, the findings may provide significant theoretical and practice implications for social work practitioners and for individuals who have been exposed to domestic violence who may receive their services" (p. 422).

Exemplar #3: Like the other examples, Yan's study of cultural tensions in cross-cultural social work practice (2008a) begins with a clear statement that theory in this area is needed. "Conceptually, a coherent framework for understanding cultural tension in cross-cultural social work practice is missing" (p. 319). Yan also ties his theoretical findings to social work practice in the conclusion: "Theoretical articulation with empirical evidence is needed for the social work profession to better handle the issues of cultural tension" (p. 327).

Fit with Symbolic Interaction Concepts

Grounded theory was developed out of symbolic interaction theory and was designed to study interactions between individuals and their social environments. This is not to say that other qualitative methodologies are inappropriate for studying such questions, but grounded theory is an especially good choice for studies at this level of analysis. For example, grounded theory can be an excellent methodology to gain understanding of individuals who are negotiating a new social environment, such as immigrants, individuals newly diagnosed with an illness, or those with changing social status (upward or downward social mobility). Early Chicago School studies focused on groups that are defined socially as "deviant" in some way, such as those with stigmatized identities (Goffman, 1963). Strauss and Glaser's original research studied patients who were dying in hospitals (Glaser & Strauss, 1965, 1968). Strauss later collaborated with former students to study persons with chronic illness (1984). He and Corbin explored the role of the caregiver of people with a serious chronic illness (Corbin & Strauss, 1988). Charmaz's work is on how the "self" changes in someone with serious chronic illness (Charmaz, 1993). All of these studies focus on the interaction between the "self" and the social environment.

Because of the foundation of grounded theory in symbolic interaction theory, problems that cannot be framed at the mezzo level of "person in environment" may not be well suited to grounded theory techniques. For example, a problem that has no social component could be difficult using grounded theory because people are not necessarily good informants concerning biologic or intrapsychic processes. Of course, studies of their ideas about these processes, and how these are shaped in social interactions, are definitely suitable. Grounded theory methods may not be productive in fields using a medical model, not only because of the consensus in the field (discussed earlier), but also because in these models, the person is not viewed as an individual who takes actions to achieve goals. Instead, the focus is likely to be on diagnostic characteristics and something that is done to the person, such as in an intervention, where the person remains essentially passive. Another example would be a study in a field with a strong psychological orientation, such as a model based on individual developmental stages. See Wells (1995) for an excellent discussion of this issue.

Each of the three exemplar grounded theory studies focuses on a problem that can be easily described using symbolic interaction concepts.

Exemplar #1: Alaggia's focus clearly reflects a symbolic interactionist perspective. "Broad areas that were probed for impact on behavioral and emotional response included relational issues (e.g., mother-child; mother-partner), the role of culture and religion, family-of-origin dynamics (past and present), perception of self and self-esteem, and availability of social supports" (p. 43).

Exemplar #2: In the justification for their study, Anderson and Danis reject the "medical model" and its diagnostic labels for abuse survivors. They broaden the traditional definition of resiliency (i.e., competency despite enduring adversity) to include individuals' strengths that develop as a means to protect themselves from oppression. Their focus on the active use of strategies of resistance toward batterers' oppression clearly reflects a symbolic interactionist worldview.

Exemplar #3: Yan utilizes a symbolic interactionist perspective when he states that his goal was to "explain actual social process" (p. 319). His study focuses on "how social workers and their cultures interact when working with clients from different cultures" (p. 319).

Theoretical Sensitivity

Theoretical sensitivity is another important consideration for the researcher choosing a topic for a grounded theory study. Theoretical sensitivity is based, in part, on the understanding a researcher brings to the study based on personal and professional experience in the area. The researcher needs to explore theoretical sensitivity in terms of potential "researcher bias" (discussed earlier), but he or she also needs to assess potential *theoretical* bias. Theoretical sensitivity of the researcher refers not only to the ability of the researcher to understand the people and the setting under study but also to his or her ability to generate meaningful theory in this area. Glaser and Strauss (1967) argued that the researcher should be "sensitizing," that is, able to "yield a meaningful picture" and to illustrate the theory so that readers can connect it to their own experience. In *Discovery*, Glaser and Strauss (1967) indicated that only sociologists would be sufficiently familiar with sociological theory to be "sensitive" to the theoretical dimensions of the study. Both Glaser (1978) and Strauss (1987) were later critical of studies that claim to use grounded theory but that never actually develop theory, and sought to enhance the ability of researchers to see the broader dimensions of their work.

The identification of theoretical concepts and explanations relevant to the study is a critical component of a grounded theory study. To explore the theoretical sensitivity you are bringing to a study, you need to examine your theoretical understanding of the research problem. Social work researchers are sometimes unaware of their own theoretical assumptions.

Grounded theory requires the researcher to come into the study with a fairly open mind. While there is some difference between the classic grounded theory model and the more recent constructivist one (see discussion in Chapter 1), the ability to put aside one's initial perspective and be open to evidence as one interacts with the data is essential in all versions. To minimize researcher bias, I encourage my students to select a research question that they are genuinely curious about, rather than picking a question for which they think they already know the answer.

Each of the three exemplar grounded studies illustrates the concept of bringing theoretical sensitivity to the research, including personal, professional, and theoretical background.

Exemplar #1: Alaggia (2002) brought a strong clinical background with the study population to her research. She states, "The design of the present study was informed by the investigator's clinical work with families of sexually abused children, co-facilitating therapeutic groups for sexually abused adolescents, and counseling adults who have been sexually abused as children" (p. 44). Also, she began with a sampling strategy based on her literature review, which suggested that maternal support was important in cases of child sexual abuse. Her study design sought out cases identified as more and less supportive.

Exemplar #2: Anderson and Danis (2006) frame their study in theories of resilience. Prior to her study on the daughters of battered women

I am using as an exemplar, Anderson had done grounded theory research on strategies of resistance in women who experienced childhood incest. In the preface to her book *Enhancing Resilience in Survivors of Family Violence* (2010), Anderson describes her background working in a rural mental health center with child sexual abuse cases during the 1980s, in which the professional field focused on victimization as the centerpiece to individuals' identities rather than what happened to them. It was this social work practice experience that led to her challenging existing theories of trauma and recovery for survivors of family violence. Danis's experience teaching a social work course on "Contemporary Issues in Domestic Violence" also led her to question current theories.

Exemplar #3: Yan, too, brings personal and professional experience to the research. In his dissertation (Yan, 2002), on which his exemplar paper is based, Yan describes himself as "a Chinese immigrant living in a multicultural context" (p. 3). He also describes the influence of different cultural perspectives on his experience as a social worker. "Like many other social workers coming from a non-western cultural background, I questioned the cultural appropriateness of some social work values and principles, such as individuality and confidentiality and how they compromised some prevalent values that I inherited from my family" (p. 4). Yan's (2008a) literature review shows familiarity with sociological theories (e.g., organizational sociology), the history of the social work profession, and professional ethics. He also brings a broad understanding of cross-cultural issues, especially conflicts between Western and non-Western worldviews.

Opportunity to Carry Out a Multistage Process That Incorporates the Key Components of Grounded Theory

Grounded theory research is based on a multistage, abductive process that incorporates theoretical sampling, constant comparison, and theoretical saturation. To do so, grounded theory researchers need access to the data (setting and population) over time, so that the iterative process of building grounded theory can take place. The grounded theory researcher continually moves back and forth between data gathering and data analysis, so that as new ideas come up (new hypotheses), additional data is gathered to explore them in more depth and see if they hold up. If you have access to data at only a single time point (e.g., some focus group studies), grounded theory techniques may be very difficult to apply.

Constant Comparative Analysis

An important characteristic of the grounded theory method is that the researcher gathers some data, makes comparisons to generate concepts, and then gathers more data to further develop the concepts and, at the same time, to verify them. By comparing case to case (whether this is individual cases or cases based on organizations or larger structures, such as societies), the researcher begins to develop "concepts." Conceptual categories are specified and described, based on constant comparison of both similarities and differences among cases. (See Chapters 3 and 4 for more detail on how this is done.)

Theoretical Sampling

Initially, sampling strategies used in grounded theory studies are similar to those used in other types of qualitative research. For example, convenience sampling is common in the initial phase of grounded theory studies. "Snowball" sampling might be used early on in a grounded theory study if a population that is "underground" is being studied. "Purposive sampling" is also appropriate at the start of a grounded theory study, when the aim is to maximize variation in the initial sample. However, as the study progresses, and as the core concepts are identified, theoretical sampling is increasingly used.

In grounded theory, the sampling framework cannot be determined in advance. To do so would risk generating a sample that is not able to further the development of the emerging theory. For example, if you decided in advance that your sample would have equal groups of social workers in public and private settings, and then your data led you to focus on something about the setting other than whether it is public or private, you might not be able to fully develop your theory because of your early sampling decision. With this type of predetermined sampling strategy, it is very difficult to avoid organizing your theory around the public/private distinction. (See Hood, 2007, for an excellent illustration of this.)

Constant comparison and theoretical sampling work hand in hand in grounded theory research. To apply both, not only do you need continued access to the data, but you will also need a sample with a wide range of characteristics and a lot of variation. That way, as the theory develops, you can explore important dimensions, properties, and relationships of your concepts.

Theoretical Saturation

Theoretical saturation means that "no additional data are being found whereby the sociologist can develop properties of the category" (Glaser & Strauss, 1967, p. 61). This means that the researcher has to be able to continue the study until there is a good fit between the theory and the data. For this reason, it can be difficult to predict how long a grounded theory study will take. Glaser and Strauss recognized that a study could go on and on without reaching saturation, and so they required that only the core category or categories be saturated. Even so, ideally a grounded theory researcher has a fairly open-ended time table. If you are working under tight time restrictions, you might have difficulty achieving the goal of theoretical saturation.

The use of a multistage research process using the key components of grounded theory is illustrated in the three exemplar studies.

Exemplar #1: Alaggia's study used a multistage process that included constant comparative analysis, theoretical sampling, and theoretical saturation in her analysis. She used the simultaneous data collection and analysis that is characteristic of grounded theory. "Grounded theory method was employed to generate hypotheses building through induction and deduction, and using the constant comparative method between more and less supportive mothers" (Alaggia, 2002, p. 43). She writes, "In keeping with grounded theory method theoretical sampling was followed where-in respondents were selected two or three at a time, based on evolving variables such as level of maternal support, maternal history of abuse, nature of relationship with the perpetrating partner, ethnic affiliation, etc." (p. 43). Finally, she states, "Saturation was reached when ten participant interviews were completed and analyzed, at which point an enormous amount of data were collected" (p. 45).

Exemplar #2: Anderson and Danis's study (2006) also used a multistage grounded theory process employing the tools of constant comparison, theoretical sampling, and theoretical saturation. They started with "initial purposive sampling criteria" (eligibility), followed by theoretical sampling. "Subsequent theoretical sampling was based on the qualitative criteria (citations) of saturation of the code categories, relevance to the emerging theory, and added variation of perspective (e.g., the sample's diversity with regard to the characteristics of the batterers' abuse)" (p. 422).

Exemplar #3: Yan's study of cross-cultural social work (2008a) explicitly used the constant comparative method. "The constant comparison method was used to analyze the data from coding, problem development, and theory building in this study. . . . In this study, because of the programmed variations in sampling focus, comparisons were made not only between different interviews, but also between data collected in different stages" (p. 330). Yan also describes how he incorporated three rounds of theoretical sampling. "In each round, to test the emerging theory, different variables—particularly ethno-racial background, field of practice, and gender—were used as criteria to recruit participants" (p. 319). Yan included a table (see Figure 2.3) in his article to show his use of theoretical sampling.

In his dissertation (2002), Yan shows how constant comparison, theoretical sampling, and theoretical saturation guided his study. He describes how he developed his initial coding scheme, based on comparisons among the first round of participants. "The first coding scheme was revised as more information from the second group of participants was collected and coded. As a result of the constant comparison of first and second sets of data, a new coding scheme was developed which was again put into a comparison process through the third round of data collection, which did not lead to any major revision of the coding scheme. Instead, most of the categories were saturated with the extra information" (p. 71).

Do You Have the Right Temperament for Grounded Theory Research?

Before concluding this section, I add one additional consideration for the researcher thinking about using grounded theory. Certain personality characteristics are considered desirable for any type of qualitative research, such as flexibility, self-reflection, and the ability to work in an iterative, nonlinear way (Padgett, 2008, p. 18). All of these are also important in grounded theory research. To these I would add an interest in thinking conceptually, enjoyment of playing with ideas, a tolerance for uncertainty, and a willingness to test your ideas and to let go of those that are not supported. I suspect that my own temperament is an important

Field of Practice	Self-identified
Round One	
Hospital	Jewish-Canadian, white
Rehabilitation institution	Ukrainian-Canadian, white
Children rehabilitation institution	Caucasian, English Quebecquor,
Hospital	Canadian with a German origin,
Mental health institution	Caucasian from Newfoundland,
Hospital	Jewish Canadian, white
Round Two	
Youth rehabilitation institution	African Canadian,
Community agency	Sri Lankan Tamil
Child protection	Chinese Canadian
Employment service	Jamaican
Settlement service	South Asian Canadian
Child mental health	Chinese-Canadian
Hospital	Indian
Privatized rehabilitative service	Chinese Canadian
Family service	Iranian-Canadian
Child protection	Black
Round Three	
Children group home	White with a Scottish origin
Settlement service	White with a Scottish origin
Child protection	Spanish speaking immigrant
Mental health	Christian Iranian
Senior home and child protection	White (Anglo-Saxon origin)
Child protection	Indian
Community health	Iranian Canadian
Mental disability	Italian Canadian
Community children mental health	Portuguese Canadian
Day program for women with trauma	Portuguese Canadian
Men committed violence against women	Latino American
Community health	Caribbean
Children rehabilitation residential	Italian
Hospital	Chilean-Canadian

Source: Yan (2008)

Figure 2.3 Theoretical sampling illustration.

factor in why I love the grounded theory method. According to the Myers-Briggs test, I am an Introverted, Intuitive, Thinking, Perceiving temperament (Quenk, 2009). My type (INTP) is described as a thinker who enjoys defining concepts; identifying patterns, causes, and consequences; and putting things into a broader context. All of these are important in the grounded theory process. As an introvert, I am comfortable spending a lot of time pouring over data. Intuition in this model means focusing on larger, abstract patterns rather than details. Thinking means that I focus more on cognitive rather than emotional aspects. Being a "perceiving" instead of a "judging" type makes me comfortable letting go of initial ideas, postponing deciding on a final scheme for the theory, and always being willing to continue seeking a better way. (This characteristic can be extremely frustrating to my colleagues and students with different temperaments.) I realize, too, that each of these also has the potential to be detrimental in my research. While I don't know of any research on this, I think there are many people who find the grounded theory method very frustrating.

Reshaping a Problematic Idea into a Good Grounded Theory Prospect

When a proposed study does not seem to be an ideal fit with the characteristics of grounded theory discussed above, it is often possible to reshape the research problem so that it can be successfully addressed using grounded theory methods. Sometimes a problematic research question can be revised to avoid a potential problem. Box 2.3 provides an example of a project idea that started with an inappropriate question and a strong potential for researcher bias.

In some cases, the methodology of a proposed project can be altered to address a potential concern. For example, problems using grounded theory in settings with strong interpretative frameworks can sometimes

---

Box 2.3 Example of Shaping of a Student's Research Question

One of my students came to me with the idea of doing a study on the question of gay parenting. She was gay, and was considering having a child herself. With some discussion, it was clear that her goal in doing this study was to show that gay couples make good parents. The research question was not a true "question" in this case, because the student was already certain that she knew the answer to the question. She was not coming to the study with an ability to see different views. On top of her lack of an open mind, her question suggested that qualitative research was not an appropriate methodology because it was a "variance" question. But grounded theory was an especially poor choice because she most likely would not be able to generate theory from the data, and would be in danger of forcing her own strong views on her data.

I helped her to change the focus of her topic so that it was a better fit with the grounded theory model. She ended up with an outstanding project on the process lesbian couples go through in deciding whether or not to have children.

be overcome if the design incorporates "prolonged engagement" (i.e., the researcher is involved over a long time period). An example is provided by a study in which the researcher conducted three interviews, over a considerable time period, with a respondent who had gone through a 12-step program. Late in the study, the respondent was shown an interview from the time when she was active in the program, and told the researcher, "I can't believe I laid that trip on you!" Because the researcher stayed with the respondent through the process and afterward, she was able to get a valid "insider perspective," including the respondent's perspective on her own experience with the recovery program. (See Chapter 5 for a discussion of mechanisms that can be built into the design to deal with potential problems.)

Another option when a researcher wants to use a grounded theory methodology but cannot meet the various criteria described in this chapter is to use as many grounded theory procedures as possible. (See Chapter 6 for a discussion on modified models of grounded theory and models in which grounded theory is combined with other methods, qualitative and quantitative.)

DESIGNING A GROUNDED THEORY STUDY

While a number of excellent texts are available to the new grounded theory researcher, there is little in these texts on study design and proposal development (Birks & Mills, 2011; Charmaz, 2006; Corbin & Strauss, 2008). In the Chicago School model, the researcher went out to explore an area of interest without much preparation (the "get your feet wet" school). Few researchers today are given the freedom to just "jump in," and a clear design, illustrated in a strong research proposal, is essential. Fortunately, when designing a grounded theory study, researchers can adapt models that have been developed for generic qualitative studies. For example, I advise my students to adapt the model developed by Maxwell (2005). This model is made up of two connected triangles (see Figure 2.4).

The top triangle is made up of three components: "Goals," "Conceptual Framework," and "Research Questions." The bottom triangle connects the "Research Questions" to the components of "Methods" and "Validity." (The first four components are discussed in this chapter.

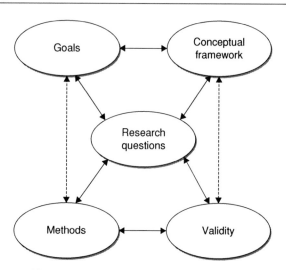

Figure 2.4 Maxwell's model for qualitative research design. Source: Maxwell (2005, p. 5).

Validity is discussed in Chapter 5.) Maxwell calls his model "interactive," because each component has implications for the others and the components have to fit together tightly. Since qualitative research studies change as they progress, when any of the components change, the researcher needs to return to the model and change the other components so that the good "fit" is reestablished. Although the model was not developed with grounded theory in mind, each of Maxwell's components is applicable to grounded theory studies. A grounded theory proposal should include the following sections: 1. Study goals, 2. Conceptual framework, 3. Research question, 4. Methods, and 5. Discussion of ethical and trustworthiness issues (see Box 2.4). (Ethical issues in grounded theory are not discussed in this volume, because they are essentially the same as for all qualitative research. The reader is advised to see qualitative texts, such as Padgett [2008] and Maxwell [2005], for a discussion of ethical issues needing consideration.)

Goals of the Study

The study goals or purpose shows why the study is important. Many possible research questions are interesting, but not important or worth the

---

Box 2.4 The Grounded Theory Proposal

- Study goals
- Conceptual framework/theoretical sensitivity
  - Personal experience
  - Professional experience
  - Relevant theories
  - Literature review
- Methods
- Trustworthiness and ethical considerations

---

time, effort, and cost of studying. In the research proposal, the goals section makes a case for why the study is worth doing, worth funding, or worth reading. Padgett (2008) calls this the "so what?" question, and emphasizes that it is the responsibility of the researcher to make the case for the study. The goals provide a justification for the study and drive all elements of the study design.

In social work, the study goals are usually related to a problem in social work practice, but other factors (e.g., funding availability, career opportunities) may also play a role. A grounded theory study should also have a goal of developing or advancing theory. The researcher should justify the choice of grounded theory method because there is a need for theory in the area. In social work research, it is important to show clearly how theory development might help social workers or policy makers.

Conceptual Framework

The "conceptual framework" is very similar to the concept of "theoretical sensitivity" in grounded theory research. The conceptual framework includes the researcher's personal or professional experience with the topic, relevant theory, and review of research (literature review).

Personal and Professional Experience

In grounded theory, your own personal and professional experience is an important component of your "theoretical sensitivity," adding to your understanding of the problem and enhancing your ability to make sense of your data. It can also be a source of researcher bias (see Chapter 5). I highly recommend doing a "researcher identity memo" (Maxwell, 2005). This goes well beyond simply describing your own background and requires you to think through how your background has shaped your thinking about the research question. Maxwell (2005) provides several examples of this kind of memo.

Relevant Theory

In this section of the "conceptual framework," you present theoretical perspectives that shape your worldview. A review of relevant theories (or conceptual models) can increase "theoretical sensitivity" by increasing awareness of significant theoretical concepts that may arise in the study. This is especially important for social work researchers, who are often not well versed in social science theory. This means that when you analyze your data, you may be less likely to see connections to theory, which can lead to a theory that is not very abstract. The important point in a grounded theory study is to review theoretical perspectives or models without allowing this initial work to blind you to new ways of looking at your data as the study progresses. Keep any theories or concepts from your review in the back of your mind, so that as you move into data collection and analysis, they can be drawn upon as needed, but avoid getting attached to any of them.

As the study progresses, most likely, concepts will arise that were not considered in the initial proposal, and you may need to explore areas of theory that were not in your conceptual framework. I provide an example in Box 2.5. In my study of daughters of women with breast cancer, I focused my theoretical discussion and literature review around the idea of risk, because I expected the daughters to be fearful of inheriting breast cancer. As I began to gather my data, however, I found that the daughters were dealing with unresolved grief, and that risk was much less important to them. As I analyzed my data, I realized that the theories of risk I had studied were not relevant to my research. At that point, I began to explore theories of grief and loss.

Literature Review

The literature review has been a controversial issue in grounded theory. In the original grounded theory model, Glaser and Strauss (1967) advised researchers not to do a literature review prior to beginning data gathering and analysis. They feared that the researcher would be tempted to "force" his or her empirical observations to fit the findings of the literature review, while new ideas and directions in the data could be overlooked. Instead, they argued that the researcher should come in with a

Box 2.5 Illustration of "Conceptual Framework"

An example from the work of one of my doctoral students can be used to illustrate the conceptual framework in grounded theory studies. Eunice Park -Lee was interested in the Korean elderly. She was concerned that many program evaluation studies in gerontology used instruments that had been developed with Western populations to measure "quality of life." Park Lee wanted to understand what "quality of life" meant for Korean immigrants to the United States. She proposed a grounded theory study based on interviews and observations. She was of Korean-American background herself. Her Korean family background added to her theoretical sensitivity for this study, as did her previous social work experience with the Korean elderly and her knowledge of theories of gerontology.

In addition to a discussion of her background, she reviewed several theoretical perspectives that might prove pertinent to her study, including disengagement theory, developmental theory of aging, stress theory, and assimilation theory. She did not see her own study as a test of these theories, nor did she limit her interviews to the areas that had been studied previously. To do this, she had to keep an open mind. She was genuinely interested in how her respondents defined "quality of life," and she was neither committed to nor opposed to any of the theoretical perspectives.

Using grounded theory procedures, over time she developed two core concepts, "creating harmony" and "creating happiness," that defined a "good life" for the Korean elderly (Park-Lee, 2005). These factors did not fit with any of the theories that were originally in her conceptual framework. In her final chapter, Park-Lee discussed how the "middle range" theory that she developed related (and did not relate) to the theories she started with. She then explored theories more related to Asian philosophical worldviews, described in the fields of religion and philosophy, not gerontology.

"blank slate" and allow the (grounded) theory to emerge from the data. Once the theory has "emerged," it is appropriate for the researcher to look into other research (and theories) to see how they fit with his or her findings. Although Glaser still advocates this approach, most grounded theory researchers today address their original concern as a type of researcher bias. In my view, not doing a literature review does not eliminate researcher bias. Also, not doing a literature review could actually reduce theoretical sensitivity. As Dey (1993) points out, an "open mind" is not the same thing as an "empty mind." From a practical stand-point, literature reviews are essential in most dissertation proposals, institutional review board (IRB) proposals, grant proposals, and publications (see Chapter 6).

Integrating the Conceptual Framework

The conceptual framework for the study can be integrated through the device that Maxwell calls a "concept map." The idea is to develop a "map" of what you speculate might be important concepts in your study. This should be based on what you think is going on. This should be a difficult process, and something that will change as you work on it. Today, there are software programs (e.g., Microsoft PowerPoint, Inspiration) that can help you to do this. An old-fashioned paper and pencil or a whiteboard is just as useful. Be sure to keep copies of your concept map, so that you can trace the development of your ideas. (If you use a whiteboard, you may want to photograph your diagrams.) One reason that it is so important to do this at the start of a study is that you (and others) can later look back and see the extent to which your initial perceptions may have influenced the analysis. When, at the end of a study, you are asked a question like, "Yes, but isn't this all stuff you knew when you started?" you can counter, "No, my ideas have changed" and show evidence from your "conceptual framework." This is an important piece of the "audit trail," discussed in Chapter 5.

Research Question

Developing a research question can be a source of considerable anxiety, especially in students who are new to qualitative research. There is a perception that there is only one RIGHT way to develop a research question, or that once the research question is stated, you are committed to it for the rest of the study. This may stem from previous training in quantitative research. In qualitative research studies, including grounded theory, the research question is initially stated as a broad area of interest, and it is only when the study progresses that a specific focus becomes clear. The research question is not something set in concrete, but rather something that reflects a starting point. It can be expected to change during the course of the research, as the researcher focuses the study. Grounded theory texts (e.g., Strauss & Corbin, 1990) have emphasized that at first, a research question can simply be the name of the substantive area you want to study. "The research question in a qualitative study is a statement that identifies the topic area to be studied and tells the reader what there is about this particular topic that is of interest to the researcher" (Corbin & Strauss, 2008, p. 25). The "question" can be simply, "What is the experience of [your study population]?" or "What's going on here?"

Qualitative research questions focus on process, and often are framed in terms of questions using words such as "how?" and "why?" In grounded theory studies, symbolic interactionist concepts can help frame the research questions. For example, because this theoretical model is based on action strategies people use to negotiate their social environments, questions often take forms like: "How do women manage the symptoms of chronic illness?" or "How, when, why, and with whom do ill people talk about their conditions, and when do they remain silent?" (Charmaz, 2006 pp. 16–17). Blumer called these symbolic interactionist concepts "sensitizing concepts" (Blumer, 1969). However, these are seen as starting points, and should not keep you from moving in other directions as you begin data gathering and analysis. What is important in grounded theory is to let the data structure the research question, and not vice versa.

Methods

The key point with respect to methods in a grounded theory study is that the data gathering must allow for the application of a multistage model incorporating the techniques of constant comparison, theoretical sampling, and theoretical saturation. In your study design, you need to incorporate opportunity to gather data, begin analysis, return to the data, use theoretical sampling to search for data that fills out emerging categories, and continue this process until a point of theoretical saturation is reached.

Like most qualitative studies, grounded theory research utilizes interviews or observations (or both) as the basic tools of data gathering. The difference is that everything that is done in grounded theory is done to further theory development. As discussed above, this focus affects the way data is gathered, because decisions about what further data to gather are driven by theoretical questions.

In the early phase of a grounded theory study, the questions in the interview may be very broad. For example, in my research on women whose mothers had breast cancer, I began with, "I understand your mother had breast cancer. Tell me about how that was for you." As I went through the process of open coding, axial coding, and selective coding (described in the following two chapters), I focused my interviews around emerging issues, such as "strategies for surviving" in the period following mothers' death. I tried to stay open to new ideas and to avoid just searching for verification of my ideas. As patterns emerged, I asked more detailed questions about them when they arose in an interview. If the concepts that were becoming important to my theory did not arise naturally in an interview, then I might ask about them. I avoid asking leading questions, but when something I am expecting to arise in an interview is not mentioned, I want to be sure that it actually didn't occur, and not that it was just was not mentioned by the respondent. In this case, I also explore the conditions that might have made this case different from other cases in the study (Oktay, 2004, 2005).

Focus groups are popular today, but in order to use them in a grounded theory model, the researcher has to be able to arrange additional focus groups as the theory develops. This can be more difficult than seeking a different person or a different setting. However, focus groups can be used very productively in grounded theory when they are used in combination with other data-gathering techniques. For example, they can be used to explore a concept that has emerged in a grounded theory analysis with a group, to validate a theory, or to fill in a dimension of a core concept.

CHAPTER SUMMARY

In this chapter I discussed the process a researcher should go through to decide if grounded theory is a good choice for his or her research project. The first question to consider is whether the research question is appropriate for qualitative research, since grounded theory is a qualitative research method. Then, I reviewed the characteristics and key components of grounded theory, so that a researcher could determine whether they are applicable to the proposed study. These key components were illustrated using the three social work grounded theory exemplars. Finally, I showed how to develop a grounded theory proposal, using an adaption of Maxwell's model (2005). In the next chapter, I show how to begin data analysis using the grounded theory method.

SUGGESTED EXERCISES

1. Identify three quantitative studies and three qualitative studies in your field of interest. Compare the research questions. Can you use Maxwell's (2005) distinction between a variance question and a process question to distinguish them?
2. Practice developing qualitative research questions, and discuss them with others to see if you can improve them. Try applying symbolic interactionist concepts and see if that helps you to formulate more interesting research questions.
3. Identify a qualitative study that does not use the grounded theory method and one that does. How are they different? How are they similar?
4. For your own research project, write a research proposal for a grounded theory study. Identify the study goals and your conceptual framework, and then write a research question. What type of methodology (e.g., data-gathering strategy) could you use to study this question?

3

Early Data Analysis

This chapter focuses on the first level of data analysis in grounded theory. In this "first step," the researcher uses line-by-line coding to begin to identify concepts from raw data. The chapter includes examples of open coding, designed to help readers to use open coding with their own data. I illustrate how the grounded theory method creates concepts that are closely tied to data. I also show how to further develop these concepts by identifying their dimensions and properties, and how to consolidate concepts into larger categories. I show how the authors of the exemplar social work grounded theory studies used the dimensions and properties of their categories in their analyses. I emphasize the importance of writing memos, even in this early stage of analysis. I illustrate how open coding and memoing further the use of the constant comparative method and theoretical sampling in grounded theory data analysis. These components of the grounded theory method help the researcher to move the analysis beyond description and toward theory building. Exercises in early analysis are provided.

EARLY ANALYSIS REFLECTS THE CORE COMPONENTS AND AIMS OF GROUNDED THEORY

Early data analysis in grounded theory must be understood within the context of the entire grounded theory process. The focus on theory development is key. Although the early coding in grounded theory may appear very similar to coding in other qualitative methods, it differs for the researcher because the ultimate goal of developing theory is never out of the researcher's mind. Some researchers make the mistake of equating the coding procedures of grounded theory with the grounded theory method. They fail to incorporate these coding steps into a multistage process for developing theory. When the coding steps (moving from concrete open coding to more abstract categories or themes) are used without the other components of grounded theory, the result is not a true grounded theory study. The key components of grounded theory, discussed in the previous chapter (theoretical sensitivity, constant comparative method, theoretical sampling, and theoretical saturation), are all reflected even in the earliest stage of grounded theory data analysis. The researcher brings theoretical sensitivity to the early coding, which reflects his or her personal, professional, and theoretical background and concepts discussed in any literature review. The early comparisons made between cases in the study (constant comparison) will lead to the development of concepts that will guide the next round of sampling (theoretical sampling). Glaser and Strauss (1967) write,

> Coding . . . should keep track of the comparison group in which the incident occurs. To this procedure we add the basic, defining rule for the constant comparison method: *while coding an incident for a category, compare it with the previous incidents in the same and different groups coded in the same category.* . . . This constant comparison of the incidents very soon starts to generate theoretical properties of the category. The analyst starts thinking in terms of the full range of types or continua of the category, its dimensions, the conditions under which it is pronounced or minimized, its major consequences, its relation to other categories and its other properties. (p. 106)

Initial coding carries significant weight in the study by impacting the direction the study will take. Even theoretical saturation, which is unlikely to occur in the early stages of data analysis, is still relevant, because this early coding will identify concepts that the researcher will ultimately aim to saturate, as well as the characteristics of these concepts.

The key difference between data analysis at the beginning of a grounded theory study and late-stage data analysis is that in the early stages, the focus of the study is not yet apparent. In fact, one function of the early coding is to narrow the scope of the study. Also, while early data analysis stays very close to the data and is more concrete, later data analysis becomes more focused and more abstract (see Chapter 4).

How Grounded Theory Analysis Differs from Other Types of Qualitative Research

The first step of analysis in grounded theory ("open coding") is the most similar to the data analysis done in other qualitative methods. Most, but not all, qualitative methods begin data analysis by coding, or breaking down and splitting up the data. Exceptions include narrative analysis, where the story is kept intact, along with very precise and detailed information about how the story is told (Wells, 2011). In phenomenological analysis, coding would be seen to disrupt the meaning and the context provided by the interview. At the other end of the continuum, some qualitative models (e.g., content analysis) set up the coding scheme in advance of the data gathering (Crabtree & Miller, 1992). This type of coding is not done in grounded theory because it increases the likelihood of "forcing" the data into preexisting categories that are not grounded in the data.

Grounded theory also differs from other qualitative methods in that data gathering and data analysis are integrated in the grounded theory method. Grounded theory involves a multistage process, and data analysis is incorporated into even the earliest stages of the study. The reverse is also true—that is, data gathering continues until very late in the study, in multiple cycles of data gathering and data analysis (theory building and theory testing). I am sometimes approached by researchers who have already completed their data gathering (e.g., interviews) who ask me how to analyze the data using the grounded theory method. This question indicates that they do not understand the interplay between data gathering and data analysis in grounded theory.

Substantive and Theoretical Codes

"Coding" means assigning data to "codes," which are simply words that are used to convey meaning. Glaser and Strauss (1967) distinguished between two types of codes that develop in the early stage. "Substantive" codes are codes that use the words and ideas of the respondents (or if observation if being used, the words, behaviors, and ideas of those being observed). When the name of the substantive code is actually in the data, the code would now be called an "in vivo" code. For example, if the respondent says, "I was overwhelmed," then the researcher might code this text "overwhelmed." Not all substantive codes are "in vivo," but they all closely reflect the raw data.

The second type of code, called a theoretical code, does not come directly from the data, but from the analyst who is doing the coding. Due to the conceptual background of the researcher, he or she will see some statements or behaviors as illustrations of theoretical concepts. For example, if a respondent says, "I immediately called my mother to talk," the researcher might code this as "social support." Theoretical codes can be problematic in grounded theory because there is a fear that the analyst will force his or her data into preexisting categories and, hence, will not be able to see beyond the prevailing paradigms in his or her field. In the initial stage of coding in grounded theory, it is important to stay very close to the data and to the worldview of the respondents. However, theoretical ideas will occur to you, and once they do, it is better to create theoretical codes immediately than to try to ignore these thoughts. These theoretical codes that are created in early coding should be treated with caution. Glaser (1978) recommended making theoretical codes "earn their way" into the analysis, meaning that you need to be certain that they are supported by the data. Creating these theoretical codes early can help the researcher to discover which theoretical perspectives he or she is bringing to the research. (Some of the methods of increasing trustworthiness in grounded theory studies discussed in Chapter 5 can be used by the researcher to ensure that theoretical concepts are supported by the data.)

BEGINNING OPEN CODING

"Open coding," the first step in coding, is a lot of fun if you come to the data with a clear and alert mind—full of curiosity and excitement. Open coding usually involves line-by-line coding. In their 1967 book, Glaser and Strauss said very little about how to do coding, other than to place it in the context of the theory-building process using constant comparative analysis. It was in later work, and most specifically in Strauss's books with Juliet Corbin, that explicit instructions on doing open coding were provided to grounded theory researchers.

In the beginning of a study, you should code everything even if it seems insignificant, since you don't know at this point where your theory will take you. Things that initially seem tangential may later turn out to be important to your theory. It is helpful to code quickly, and not to think too deeply as you code—especially the first run-through. This will help you to avoid any forcing. It is important not to let yourself jump quickly to an abstract theoretical level. Treat these theoretical codes as hypotheses or questions that may or may not be helpful as you continue your analysis (see Box 3.1).

Problems in Open Coding

Students sometimes have difficulty with open coding, questioning whether they are doing it "right." This reflects an inappropriate application of the concept of "interrater reliability" used in quantitative research. In grounded theory, there is no one right way to code. Different coders will do it somewhat differently, depending on what they are bringing to the study. This is to be expected, and does not constitute a problem. I find that multiple coders will usually produce fairly consistent results (see exercise #2). I see coder differences as an opportunity for discovering more nuanced meanings. Discussion of these differences can lead to discoveries that advance the theory. (See discussion of CAQDAS in Chapter 6 on coder reliability.)

When social workers with clinical backgrounds code, there can be a tendency to apply diagnostic labels to respondents, such as "depression"

Box 3.1 Tips for Open Coding
• Code words and phrases that describe or evoke strong emotions. • Code words and segments that describe actions (Glaser recommends using gerunds—that is, verbs ending with "-ing"-to emphasize actions). • Code material that reflects symbolic interaction concepts, such as sense of self, expectations of social roles, assessment of the judgments of others, and justifications for actions. • Look for "red flags," such as phrases that reflect assumptions ("everyone knows," "always," "never").

and "denial." When you are trying to understand the respondent's world-view, a clinical background can lead to a "trained incapacity." You need to stay close to what the respondents actually say, how they think, and how they describe their feelings. If you find that you cannot see past a diagnostic perspective, this may not be a good area for you to do this type of research. If you decide to continue with a study close to your clinical work, it is important to build in mechanisms (discussed in Chapter 5) that will help you to see beyond the clinical perspective.

An Illustration of Open Coding

An illustrative example may be helpful. Below is an excerpt from an interview that was done in 1988 with a mother whose son had died from AIDS. The first paragraph of her interview follows.

Interview Segment to Illustrate Open Coding

Well let me just say it would be best if we started when we visited J. in Paris. And when we went over there we were going to spend a month with him because we had been estranged from him for ten years because we didn't accept him being gay, although we loved him, we did not accept his gayness. But while we were there J. was getting neuropathy and losing the use of his hands. We were very thankful we were there at a time when he really needed us. So we brought him back to D.C. because we couldn't get him back to San Francisco and it's really better because we could take better care of him here. We had a chair lift from my mother which came in very handy for him. And of course his sisters and brothers were here. We were sorry he was away from his friends. And flying over, the person who was going through my mind to help take care of him, and the woman who came to our house to help take care of my elderly mother for about six years, Maria, I was banking on her and I thought "Oh, she'll help," but when I called Maria, she did part-time jobs 10 hours a week for an elderly woman and then did other jobs for about 5 or 6 other families. But when Maria found out that he had AIDS she did not want to come to the house, so I suggested she talk to her doctor, so she told me her doctor said it was alright, that it was hard to catch, but she told me, "You know when I told the other people about it, they told me if I came in your house I could not go on to their house." In fact she told me that one woman would not let her into her house until at least

6 to 12 months after he died. So we had a very difficult time getting help.

Figure 3.1 shows my coding of this interview segment. In my coding, I separate the different types of codes (in vivo, substantive, and theoretical codes). First, I read the interview and underline the in vivo codes. I add additional substantive codes in the right margin, and I put theoretical codes in the left margin, to clearly distinguish them from the substantive codes. (See Chapter 6 on using qualitative research software for open coding.)

I first coded the word "estranged" as an in vivo code by underlining it. This was the first word in the segment that jarred me as I read the story. Then, I put in a substantive code, "rejecting son," using my own words. I try to use gerunds when coding, as recommended by Glaser (1978) and Charmaz (2006), to focus on the respondent as an active player in the story (e.g., "experiencing loss of function," "experiencing difficulty getting help"). I also coded things that reflect symbolic interaction concepts such as justifications for actions (e.g., that she felt she could provide better care for her son at her home) and expectations of others (e.g., that Maria wouldn't help because she feared the reaction of her

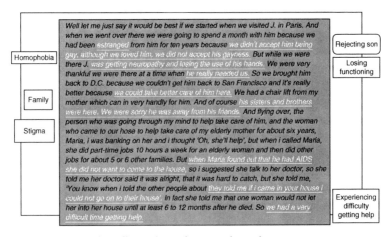

Figure 3.1 Open Coding Illustration—data to codes and concepts.

other clients). As I was coding this segment, several broader concepts jumped into my mind, so I added three theoretical codes: "homophobia," "family," and "stigma" (left side of figure). I put these codes in the left margin to remind me that these are very tentative codes and I will probably change them as the study progresses. Putting them down allows me to clear my mind and return to focusing closely on the data. Finally, I identified the respondent's idea that she could love her son without accepting his sexual identity. This suggests a complex relationship between two codes ("loved him" and "did not accept his homosexuality"). I decided to write a memo on this (see section below on memos), because it was something that I wanted to think about in more depth, and it was too complex to be handled with a simple code. (Later in the analysis I might create a category of strategies mothers used to handle the conflict between conflicting expectations.)

Concepts and Categories

The second step in open coding is to group codes into broader concepts and categories. To illustrate, here are three concepts I developed out of the interview used to illustrate open coding (with the mother whose son had AIDS) along with the codes I used to create them. (Some of these codes come from parts of the interview that were not included in Figure 3.1.)

Rejecting Son

"We didn't accept his gayness"

"We were estranged for 10 years"

"She (Maria) did not want to come to the house"

"They (Hospital) put us over in a corner. They put us away from everyone else. They segregated us really"

"We saw no one"

Taking Care

"We were very thankful we were there at a time when he really needed us"

"We could take better care of him here"

"The person who was going through my mind (Maria) to help take care of him"

"There was going to be someone come out and help with things and bathe him every morning"

"His dad and I and his brothers helped"
"And finally I said, J. I'll roll up my coat and you can lay on the couch.
That would provide some relief for you"
Difficulty Getting Help
"We had a difficult time getting help"

When coding qualitative data, it quickly becomes apparent that some codes go together. These are then combined into "concepts." For example, in the interview illustration (above), "neuropathy" can be seen as a code, which in turn could be seen as part of a larger concept: "experiencing loss of functioning." This concept could include a range of symptoms. Categories are even broader concepts created when several concepts can be grouped together. A broader category, such as "illness characteristics," might later be developed that encompassed loss of functioning, pain, threat of death, etc. The same could be done with the theoretical code "family," which could be made into a category that combined different types of family relationships.

Don't worry about whether something is a "code," a "concept," or a "category." It is somewhat arbitrary, based on how important or central the concept is to your developing theory. What is important is that you need to go from a large number of codes to a relatively small number of categories that will make up the heart of your theory. In my work, I label everything a "concept" in the early part of a study and only develop some into categories later, when I can see that they come up consistently in the data and relate to other concepts. Figure 3.2 illustrates the relationship between codes, concepts, and categories.

The process of developing categories from concepts and codes is illustrated by the work of Marlene Matarese (2010), who used grounded theory coding in an analysis of gay, lesbian, bisexual, and transgender (GLBT) youth in the foster care and juvenile justice systems. Since this was an exercise, she used data from several publications on her population. (Had this been a grounded theory study instead of a class exercise, Matarese would have returned to the field to gather additional data to dimensionalize and test these categories). Matarese began by doing substantive coding of the interview data, using gerunds where possible (see Figure 3.3).

She then created 24 concepts from her coding and after further analysis, she combined these into 12 broad categories. Figure 3.4 shows the

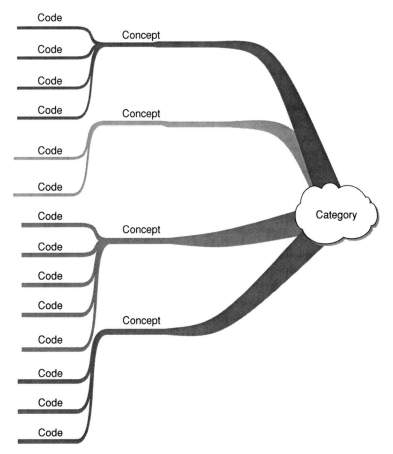

Figure 3.2 Codes, concepts, and categories.

codes and concepts that make up three of the categories she developed, "trusting others," "being and feeling safe," and "wanting to be accepted."

Developing Concept and Category Dimensions, Properties, and Subcategories

The next step in open coding is to begin identifying dimensions and properties of your concepts and categories. I see this step as part of "open coding", but it is sometimes considered to be part of "axial coding" (See Chap. 4)." It is at this point that grounded theory coding begins to differ markedly from other qualitative methods. Grounded theory analysis is

Figure 3.3   Example of Open Coding of Data on GLBT Youth in Foster Care.

based on two processes: asking questions and making comparisons. When you begin to compare cases, settings, or incidences, dimensions and properties of concepts and categories become apparent.

To illustrate the process of identifying properties and dimensions using the open coding example in Figure 3.1, consider the concept I created called "experiencing loss of functioning." The first code I identified was "neuropathy." I might begin to ask questions like, "What does the symptom neuropathy mean?" "To whom (the patient, the caregiver)?" "What other types of symptoms do people with AIDS experience?" "How would neuropathy compare to those other symptoms?" "What might be some of the dimensions of symptoms? For example, are they painful? How painful?" (That is, pain might range from no pain to extreme pain.) "What type of pain is it? Is it sharp or dull? Is it sudden,

A. "Trusting Others"

CODES	CONCEPTS	CATEGORIES
Being afraid to tell foster family "More time in the closet for me" Knowing you would not be able to tell placements you were gay Feeling like it's hard to come out because youth don't know how people are going to act especially because of multiple placements Keeping quiet so they don't find out sexual orientation Not telling first two workers about being trans or queer Not telling because I didn't feel safe with her Being scared to come out because you don't want to experience pain of rejection one more time Not wanting to share because I thought I was a freak Feeling scared to ask caseworker to introduce lesbian foster parents	Being afraid to disclose	Trusting Others
Trying to hint to caseworker about sexuality Caseworker not picking up on hints about youth sexuality Dropping hints and signals that were not picked up by caseworker Waiting for reactions when sharing information about relationships to see if they can disclose	Testing if safe to disclose	
Not being able to count on worker to find supportive foster family Believing caseworker wouldn't be able to handle youth telling her they were gay May not trust foster family	Lacking trust in adults/professionals	

Figure 3.4   Illustration of Developing Categories from Concepts and Codes.

constant, or intermittent?" In the sample interview, the son was not able to use his hands. "How does not being able to use one's hands impact functioning?"

Let's take the category "rejecting son." I would begin to ask myself questions about rejection, such as, "Are there different types or levels of

B. "Being and Feeling Safe"

CODES	CONCEPTS	CATEGORIES
Fearing for my safety Feeling afraid harassment may get out of hand Feeling like I live in hell Youth not feeling safe in placements Not telling because I didn't feel safe with her Carrying a knife to protect yourself Needing safety	Feeling unsafe	
Not having to watch your back at LGBT group home LGBT group home first place where I felt safe Feeling safe in LGBTQ group home to be myself without getting harassed Feeling safe to disclose to new work because she had a poster about gay people and rainbow beads	Feeling safe	**Being and Feeling Safe**
Needing a safe place like other youth need a safe place Not being interested in peers sexually because being safe is more important Doing anything you can to survive	Wanting to feel safe	

C. "Wanting to be Accepted"

CODES	CONCEPTS	CATEGORIES
Having a big H on juv hall record Not wanting to be branded Being labeled as different is like living with a handicap	Being labeled	
Not wanting people to think I was weird Dreaming to live in a family that accepts me Being concerned about what people say about gay people Not wanting to be weird Feeling like the odd person out Having depression, but treatment focusing on gayness	Not wanting to be different	**Wanting to be Accepted**
Feeling like youth could be themselves at LGBT group home Can be myself at LGBT group home Being able to be myself and not having to change at gay group home	Ability to be themselves	
Not wanting to share because I thought I was a freak Thinking and judging your own thoughts and how sick of a person you are Feeling like if a person really knew they wouldn't love you anymore	Internalizing negative beliefs	

Figure 3.4 (Continued)

rejection?" "What type of rejection is occurring in the case of J's mother?" Of note, the mother says both "We loved him" and "We didn't accept his gayness," suggesting that it is possible (for her) to reject some behaviors while at the same not rejecting the person. This suggests that along the dimension of "level of rejection," this mother is somewhere in the middle between complete rejection (rejection of all aspects of the person) and complete acceptance. At this stage, it is also common to create subcategories of broader categories. You can easily see that once you begin to ask questions of your concepts and categories and compare cases to each other, you will begin to see dimensions and properties.

In grounded theory, open coding begins the constant comparison process, since codes are compared and grouped into concepts and categories. As the researcher begins open coding, he or she then applies "theoretical sampling," seeking more data (cases, settings, conditions) to explore and validate the concepts that were identified in the first round. I recommend coding two or three interviews before deciding on what characteristics to seek in the next round of data collection. These new cases can then be coded and the codes and categories can be compared, generating dimensions and properties.

To reiterate, it is the data analysis I am describing (identifying concepts and categories and their dimensions and properties) that gives direction to theoretical sampling and further data gathering. In the case I have been using to illustrate, my next step might be to seek mothers whose sons had different symptoms. In the example provided in Matarese's exercise (2010), she would next think about the categories she developed (e.g., trusting others) to generate properties and dimensions. She might seek out new cases so that she has a range of "trust" in her sample. Or she might identify different types of trust or different types of "others" who are likely to be more or less trusted.

In the early stage of analysis, the researcher identifies, refines, and asks questions concerning concepts and categories. Sometimes what was originally identified as a concept is later seen to be a dimension or property of a category. For example, continuing with my illustration in Figure 3.1, one of my initial concepts was "rejecting son." But with further thought, I might create a broader category, perhaps called "reacting to son's homosexuality," which has a range from "rejecting son" at one extreme to "accepting son" at the other. I might later want to change my concept "difficulty getting care" to "getting care," with "level of difficulty" being one of its properties.

It is important not to get "hung up" on the wording used by Glaser and Strauss to identify characteristics of concepts and categories ("dimensions and properties"). These words do not always fit the nature of the data. The terms seem to reflect a positivist worldview with concepts and categories we see as "variables" that could later be tested in quantitative (or further qualitative) research. Those of a more "constructivist" bent may be uncomfortable with these terms (and aims) and may prefer to think of them as "constructions" instead of "variables." The important thing is to think about your concepts, to ask questions about them (of yourself, your colleagues, and your data), and to develop tentative answers that you can explore as you seek more data.

Examples of Concept Dimensions and Properties in the Social Work Exemplar Studies

The authors of the three exemplar social work studies introduced earlier in this volume illustrate the process of developing dimensions and properties of concepts and categories.

Examplar #1

Alaggia (2002) developed three broad categories in her study of how mothers react when they find out their daughters have been sexually abused: "belief," "affective response," and "behavioral response." She states, "However, as analysis proceeded dimensions of these categories emerged and were further elaborated as supported by the participant responses" (p. 46). "Belief" in maternal responses ranges from complete belief in the child's story to disbelief or doubt. For the category of "belief," Alaggia identified the following "dimensions":

- Mother's unconditional belief of the child's report
- Mother questions veracity of the child's report
- Mother questions identity of the perpetrator
- Mother relies on physical evidence to believe the child's report fully
- Mother questions some aspects of the child's report
- Mother does not believe the child initially
- Mother does not believe the child over time

In her analysis, Alaggia recognized that her category "belief" also had a temporal dimension. "In four of the cases, the mother's response changed over six months and this occurred in one of two directions— from supportive to less supportive *and* from less supportive to more supportive" (p. 50). That is, the dimensions of the categories were not static, but could change over time. Alaggia developed the same type of range (dimensions) for "affective support" and "behavioral support." Alaggia finds that all three of her core categories are multidimensional and that they reflect "a process that is fluid, rather than static, which changes over time so that initial and enduring response is important to discern" (p. 51).

Exemplar #2

In the Anderson and Danis paper (2006), the authors identify strategies used by the daughters of battered women. One of these strategies is called "withstand." Four specific activities are described in this category: "Creating physical and mental escapes," "Attempting to understand family dynamics," "Building support networks," and "Creating order within familial chaos." The authors elaborate their category, showing a range of ways that daughters withstand the abusive home environment.

Exemplar #3

Yan's grounded theory dissertation led to three published articles: one published earlier (2005) providing an overview of the findings, the one we have been discussing as an exemplar (2008a), and a third, also published in 2008 in *Families in Society* (2008b). In this article, Yan identifies three different types of cross-cultural interaction experienced by social workers. "Unilateral crossing" occurs when the cross-cultural process is a one-way crossing by the social worker. A second type of cross-cultural engagement, "bilateral crossing," occurs when both social worker and client cross cultural boundaries. Finally, "blending and merging" is a higher level of cross-cultural exchange, which occurs when the cultures of the social worker and the client blend or merge into something that is beyond each of the two cultures. In this example Yan shows a range of cross-cultural interactions, which not only identifies different types (properties) but also shows a range from a lower level of cross-cultural exchange to a higher level (dimensions).

MEMOS IN EARLY DATA ANALYSIS

In grounded theory, the researcher uses memos to record ideas, questions, and thoughts. It is in memoing that the key components of grounded theory are integrated. As you compare one case to the next (constant comparison), both differences and similarities should be explored and developed in memos (see Box 3.2).

Therefore, as soon as you begin to develop concepts and categories, it is important to start writing memos. Whenever ideas arise during the early coding process, stop coding and write a memo. See Box 3.3 for some tips on memo writing.

Problems with Early Memo Writing

New grounded theory researchers often wait to write down their thoughts until the end of the project, and then have great difficulty writing up their study (Charmaz, 2006). Early on, researchers may be reluctant to commit their thoughts to paper (or computer), thinking that they are not "good enough." Some researchers have a hard time writing up new ideas that are not yet well developed. Many students have been trained to only write something up when it is finished (Becker, 1998). To write memos, you may need to learn to turn the "critical" part of your brain off, so that you

---

Box 3.2 Memos in open coding

- Describe cases, settings, and incidents.
- Create and describe concepts.
- Provide in-depth analysis of concepts.
- Combine concepts into categories.
- Compare cases, settings, and incidents.
- Discuss and develop dimensions and properties of concepts and categories.
- Develop subcategories of your categories.
- Ask questions of your data, and speculate on the answers.
- Let your thinking go wherever it likes (no judgments!).

Box 3.3 Tips for memos
• Date and title each memo.
• Write memos often, throughout the data collection and analysis process.
• Do not wait to write a memo until an idea is well developed.
• Turn the critical brain off to spark creativity.
• Turn the critical brain on to analyze deeply.
• Go back and revise memos as you continue data gathering.
• Use diagrams or matrices

can think freely. It is helpful to think of writing memos as a creative process. Speculative thinking is important throughout grounded theory analysis. These early memos can be very short, and the writing style can be rough. The point is to get your ideas down before you forget them.

Others may feel that their effort will be wasted if they do a thoughtful memo on something and then later do not use it in the analysis. The fact that you have written a memo on something does not mean that it will eventually develop into a core category, or even that you will use it at all in your analysis. In grounded theory, it is important to keep an open mind. You need to be able to develop tentative ideas without committing to them. The grounded theory method involves developing tentative theoretical ideas and then testing them out through further data gathering and analysis. Many of these early ideas will not be supported as you continue through the multistage grounded theory process. However, writing memos that are later not used is not a waste of energy. Your idea is more likely to evolve than to be discarded entirely. Later, you will want to have a record of how your thinking evolved through the project.

Memoing is not limited to the early stages of grounded theory analysis. It continues throughout the study, but the focus of the memos changes (Lofland, Snow, Anderson, & Lofland, 2006). To continue with my earlier example, questioning could lead to further speculation about properties of symptoms. For example, you may find that some AIDS symptoms are visible and some invisible, affecting whether the patient and caregiver can hide the diagnosis from others. As the study progresses and new cases are brought in, additional questions and comparisons about how these new cases relate to the cases identified earlier will be explored in expanded or new memos. In her text, Charmaz provides an excellent illustration showing the progression of her ideas through her memos (Charmaz, 2006). In addition to documenting the process of developing and refining concepts and categories, when you put your thoughts "on paper," you clarify your reasoning. Also, memos provide a record of your "theory building" process. Your memos provide an audit trail that can be used to support your theory and to meet requirements of dissertation committees, funders, and IRBs.

Memoing Reflects and Guides the Next Steps of the Multistage Grounded Theory Process

In grounded theory, memoing helps you to develop your sampling strategy (theoretical sampling), because as important concepts are identified in early coding, they give direction to your next step in sampling. In the example provided earlier in the chapter, memos might suggest you look for families who were not estranged from their sons, families who did not have difficulty getting help, or mothers who did not take on caregiving for their dying sons. Memos are also important because they provide a record of your thinking process through the study and your decisions about what you want to look for in your next round of data gathering. They demonstrate how you used constant comparison, theoretical sensitivity (bringing your own experience and your theoretical framework into your analysis), and theoretical sampling to guide each step in the multistage grounded theory process.

CHAPTER SUMMARY

In this chapter, I provided an introduction to open coding, the first level of data analysis in grounded theory, including how to create in vivo, substantive, and theoretical codes from raw data; how to further develop concepts by identifying their dimensions and properties; and how to consolidate concepts into larger categories. I also discussed how the use of the "constant comparative" method and theoretical sampling helps the researcher to move the analysis beyond description and toward theory building. I emphasized the importance of beginning memo writing even at the earliest stage of analysis. Finally, I discussed how early memo writing can guide your next steps in grounded theory analysis.

SUGGESTED EXERCISES

1. Do "open coding" on some data, such as an interview transcript or field notes. (If you do not have your own data, see if you can borrow some, or find something that you can use such as a memoir.) You should code at least two to three pages of data. (If your data are extensive, select a segment that is "rich" or that has you wondering.)
   - Underline or highlight key words and phrases.
   - Use marginal codes to attach words or concepts to text.
   - Use symbolic interactionism concepts to guide your coding (i.e., code for actions the respondent is taking, look for interactions, meanings, expectations, roles, strategies).
   - Identify "red flags," emotions, and unusual words or phrases in the data.

2. Ask two or three colleagues to open code the same excerpt from your own work. Compare your coding. Is there a difference in the level of agreement in "in vivo" codes compared to more theoretical codes?

3. On the basis of your open coding, identify two or three concepts that you think might be important to understanding "what's going on here?" What might be possible dimensions or properties of these concepts? (How might they vary in other cases, other situations?)

4. Write a brief memo on the results of your open coding exercise. Was it valuable? What open coding techniques worked well for you? What didn't work? What problems did you have doing open coding? What might be important "next steps" for your project?

4

Late-Stage Analysis

This chapter focuses on the process of building theory from the concepts and categories developed in open coding (Chapter 3). In this chapter, I introduce and illustrate the concepts of axial coding and selective coding, the final stage of grounded theory coding. A variety of techniques to stimulate thinking in the later stages of coding, such as the use of matrices and diagrams, are illustrated. I emphasize how these techniques fit into the multistage abductive process of grounded theory. As with the earlier chapters, I illustrate the use of these techniques in the exemplar grounded theory social work studies. I conclude with exercises that students and researchers can use to apply the material in this chapter.

BACKGROUND

In the years following the publication of *Discovery* (1967), Glaser and Strauss were often disappointed that researchers purporting to use the grounded theory method failed to develop any theory. They did not get beyond the descriptive level in their data analysis. Since theory building is the raison-d'être of grounded theory, Glaser (1978) and Strauss (1987) wrote books that were designed to help these researchers move to a more abstract level of analysis, that is, to develop the relationships between their concepts and categories. This is how grounded theory analysis differs from thematic analysis, where the researcher identifies themes (similar to categories in grounded theory parlance) but does not attempt to relate the themes to each other. (See Chapter 5 for a discussion of Sandelowski and Barroso's typology of qualitative research [2003].)

In this chapter, I discuss a variety of techniques to help grounded theory researchers to move their analysis up to higher levels of abstraction. Some of these are discussed in grounded theory texts and some are taken from other resources. I encourage you to seek out resources, texts, and exemplars that work for you and for the particular study, as long as they help you achieve the goal of theory development, whether they call themselves "grounded theory" or not.

WORD-BY-WORD ANALYSIS

Word-by-word analysis, or microanalysis, is a technique that Strauss used in his seminars at UCSF (Corbin & Strauss, 2008; Strauss, 1987; Strauss & Corbin, 1990). It aims to stimulate more abstract thinking by focusing intensely on specific words in the data. In his seminars, Strauss takes a sentence from the data and then asks the seminar participants questions about every word in it. For example, he takes the following sentence from a field note: "She changed the blood transfusion bag," and in the discussion, brings up issues of work tasks ("changed the blood"), working alone versus with others ("she"), medical equipment and supplies ("transfusion bag"), and body invasion (Strauss, 1987). Another example is provided in the 2008 Corbin and Strauss text ("Microanalysis," pp. 58–63), consisting of a fairly lengthy discussion of the word "when" from the data fragment, "When I heard the diagnosis, it was scary." (See the transcripts of these seminars in Strauss [1987] and Corbin and Strauss [2008] to get a feel for this technique.) By focusing intensely on a single word, the researcher is pushed to go beyond his or her first impression or first interpretation and develop a broader understanding.

I use a modified version of this technique when I explore the meaning(s) of especially significant words in the data in my student seminars. Consider, for example, the transcript fragment I introduced in Chapter 3. The mother uses the word "estranged" to describe her relationship with her son. Applying the word-by-word technique, I might raise a series of questions about the word "estranged." For example, "What other words could she have used?" "How does being 'estranged' differ from these other words?" "What conditions might lead to estrangement in families?" "How might 'estrangement' differ among different relationships in the family (mother-son, father-son, mother-daughter, father-daughter, siblings)?" "How do different families handle issues of difference?" "What factors might influence how difference is handled?" or "What might be some of the consequences of estrangement in a family?" The discussion that results from this type of analysis makes the researcher think more deeply about his or her data and think in different ways that may not have occurred to him or her before. It is especially helpful to do this kind of analysis with people of different backgrounds and perspectives. This technique can raise new ideas and questions that can then be explored in the next steps of data gathering and analysis.

AXIAL CODING

Axial coding involves further exploration of categories and concepts that were developed in the process of open coding. The concept of "axial coding" was introduced by Strauss in his 1987 book, and at that time it was seen as a component of open coding rather than a separate stage of analysis. Strauss defined axial coding as "intense analysis done around one category at a time, in terms of the paradigm items (conditions, consequences, and so forth). This results in cumulative knowledge about relationships between this category and other categories and subcategories" (p. 32). The components of axial coding are (1) identifying the variety of conditions, actions/interactions, and consequences associated with a category; (2) relating a category to its subcategories; and (3) looking for clues in the data about how major categories might relate to each other. "It is unlikely to take place during the early days or even weeks when the initial data are collected and analyzed. However, axial coding becomes increasingly prominent during the normally lengthy period of open coding, before the analyst becomes committed to a core category or categories. . ." (Strauss, 1987, p. 32).

Although both Charmaz and Corbin dropped axial coding as a separate step in their most recent books, I think that axial coding can be a valuable "middle step" because it bridges the gap from open coding to selective coding. Whether axial coding is seen as a step that follows open coding or as part of open coding, the researcher is likely to be doing open and axial coding at the same time in the study, but for different concepts. That is, you might be working on axial coding for those concepts identified early in your analysis, while other concepts that continue to arise from new data sources require open coding.

Exploring Conditions and Consequences

Throughout grounded theory analysis, the researcher continues to make comparisons and to ask questions of the data, but in the advanced stage of coding, the questions asked are different from those asked earlier. Questions asked in the axial coding phase concern the context, the conditions under which something occurs, and its consequences. Glaser identified the "6 C's," consisting of cause, context, contingencies, consequences, covariance, and conditions (Glaser, 1978). Applying this to the example of mothers of sons with AIDS introduced in Chapter 3, in axial coding I would ask questions such as, "Under what conditions do parents reject their gay sons?" "What are the consequences of this?" "To whom?" I would also raise questions concerning the process (sequences of actions) by which the rejection occurs ("how" questions). Finally, I would try combining process questions (sequences of actions) with structural questions (under what conditions?) to raise more complex questions such as, "Under what conditions does the rejection start in childhood?"

In Chapter 3, I introduced Marlene Matarese's data (2010) on GLBT children in out-of-home care to illustrate open coding. Figure 4.1 shows a summary of Matarese's axial coding for the three categories whose development was shown in Figure 3.4 ("Trusting others," "Being and feeling safe," and "Wanting to be accepted"). For each category Matarese considers the causal conditions, intervening conditions, and consequences of the category. She also looks at action strategies, reflecting the symbolic interaction focus of grounded theory. Finally, she raises theoretical questions and tries out answers to the basic question, "What's going on here?"

Category	Trusting Others
Causal Conditions	Prior rejection, lack of protection, abuse, experiencing negative attitudes, not feeling supported or accepted, experiencing lack of support and acceptance, adolescence, limited support system
Intervening Conditions	Prior experiences not being protected leading to system involvement, prior experience with rejection, prior experiences where trust was broken, experiences seeing others breaching trust and outing people, seeing consequences when disclosure happens and trust is broken
Action Strategies	Being able to trust or not trust others, showing trust through self-disclosure about sexual orientation, showing trust through self-disclosure about being in foster care, trusting that her placement would continue if she comes out
Consequences	Silence, shame, isolation, fear, stigma, rejection, peer rejection or building relationships, experiencing unconditional support, feeling "normal" and accepted, discovering pride in self
Theoretical Questions/What's going on here?	Do youth in out-of-home care as a whole have issues around trust? How does this look different for sexual minority youth? Do sexual minority youth in out-of-home care have negative experiences where trust is broken? What does that breach of trust look like for sexual minority youth in out-of-home care? Do trust issues result from a fear of rejection and appear through lack of disclosure to others about one's self?

Category	Being and Feeling Safe
Causal Conditions	Not being protected, experiencing abuse and violence, being made to feel different, being humiliated, not being supported, being supported, adult behaviors based on stereotypes, rejection, lack of permanency
Intervening Conditions	Prior experiences not being protected leading to system involvement, system structures, organizational culture, lack of education for protectors
Action Strategies	Youth searching for safe people to disclose, carrying a knife, isolating, running away, detaching or not attaching, opening up in safe places, being self, coming out
Consequences	Continually feeling unsafe, feeling unable to control their lives, bodies, sexuality; feeling and experiencing powerlessness, building mistrust, reinforcing that they can't trust adults to protect, feeling a lack of support, internalizing negative attitudes toward sexual minorities, depression, suicide, alcohol/substance abuse, being allowed to be physically and mentally harmed, feeling rejected, feeling safe, having a sense of pride, developing relationships with supportive adults and peers
Theoretical Questions/What's going on here?	Do all youth who are in out-of-home settings have concerns about being safe? Is it prior experiences that first develop feelings around safety? Do nonsexual minority youth also experience feeling unsafe in care? It seems again like safety is directly connected to whether a youth is protected and supported and can be free to disclose SM status. Youth who felt supported and protected in the system and their living environments described feeling safe.

Category	Wanting to be Accepted
Causal Conditions	Feeling like they are not accepted or will not be accepted based on prior experiences, feeling accepted when supported and safe
Intervening Conditions	Don't all young people want to be accepted?
Action Strategies	Not disclosing unless it is safe, isolating, distancing, searching for safe accepting place
Consequences	Being able to be self, wanting to be self, being afraid to be self, disclosure, fear of being branded and labeled, being labeled, feeling alone
Theoretical Questions/What's going on here?	Not being accepted because of stereotypes can lead to silencing and mistrust for youth as well as internalizing negative attitudes and feeling unsafe and unprotected.

Figure 4.1 Axial coding exercise.

Relating Concepts and Categories to One Another

Advanced grounded theory analysis focuses on developing the relationships between the concepts and categories in the theory. One technique is to link them at the level of properties and dimensions. To illustrate using the mothers of sons with AIDS study, my early analysis identified three concepts: "rejecting son," "taking care," and "difficulty getting help."

To explore the connection between these categories, I would consider how the type and level of rejection might impact the mothers' experience of caretaking and the difficulty in getting help. Suppose that in open coding I had identified one of the properties of "rejecting son" to be the source of the rejection, with the possibility of rejection by the family or rejection by the community, or both. In axial coding, I might hypothesize that when rejection by the family is stronger, "taking care" might be harder for the family, while when rejection by the community is stronger, there might be more "difficulty getting help."

This type of hypothesis generating is initially fairly speculative. To verify my hypothesis, I would use these ideas to guide my next round of data gathering using theoretical sampling. I would try to seek out cases that represented a range of levels of rejection (dimensions) and a range of properties of rejection (such as the source of rejection, whether or not it is openly expressed, whether it is reciprocated, etc.). Next, I would seek cases that represent the more likely and unlikely outcomes, according to my hypothesis. In this way, the researcher uses abductive logic, moving back and forth between theory generation and theory testing (see the example provided at the end of this chapter).

Matrices

One way to interrelate categories is to use matrices, a technique used by Glaser and Strauss in their work on dying, to show how categories relate to each other. An example from my "daughters study" (Oktay, 2005) would be the matrices I developed for the four age groups I identified to define the "age" category. I also identified another category, made up of a set of distinct "stages" that demarked the daughter's experience: the period during the mother's illness and treatment, the period after the mother's death, and the long term. Putting the age groups in a matrix with the three stages created a matrix with 12 cells (see Figure 4.2).

I then examined the data in each of these cells, and from these data, I identified additional concepts for each cell of the matrix. Figure 4.3 shows the matrix that I created for the four age groups for the stage "after mother's death."

Creating these matrices facilitated my thinking about how the categories in my analysis were (or were not) related to each other. Figure 4.3 shows different patterns for each cell in the matrix. By using this technique, I identified two new categories: "adapting to family changes" and

Age groups

Stages	Children	Young adolescents	Late adolescents	Young adults
During illness and treatment				
After mother's death				
Long term				

Figure 4.2 Creating a matrix out of two categories ("daughters study").

"surviving." These new categories were then compared and contrasted in the data to see if the hypothesis (e.g., "children try to appear tough to survive") holds up as new data were gathered.

A classic sourcebook compiled by Miles and Huberman (1994) is very useful for illustrating how to use matrices to develop relationships among categories. The data displays provided in the sourcebook suggest different ways that categories can be related to each other. Studying these examples can suggest new ways for looking at data and help to identify the nature of the relationships among categories and concepts in your theory. Although not labeled "grounded theory," the types of matrices

	Adapting to Family Changes	Surviving
Children	Adapting to a Cinderella family	Surviving by being tough
Young Adolescents	Handling difficult relationships with fathers	Surviving by being like everyone else (peer group)
Late Adolescents	Handling oedipal issues with fathers	Surviving through survival of the family
Young Adults	Taking charge of family changes	Surviving through healthy grieving

Figure 4.3 Filling in a matrix ("daughters" example). Source: Oktay (2005).

presented in the sourcebook help the researcher explore relationships between categories and concepts in a grounded theory study.

Moving to Higher Levels of Abstraction

An important component of grounded theory analysis involves the attempt to move your developing theory to a higher level of abstraction. One way to do this is to tie your theory to broader social science theory. Glaser's 1978 book introduced the concept of "coding families" to help researchers apply basic social science concepts to their theories. Perhaps because this technique requires the researcher to possess a solid background in social science theory, it has not been widely used. Not many social work researchers have the broad familiarity with social science theories that Glaser and Strauss brought to their own research.

"Social science framing" described by Lofland and his colleagues (2006) has a similar goal. They identify eight basic questions that, when applied to your categories, can further the grounded theory analysis. The questions are:

1. What are the types?
2. How often does this occur (frequencies)?
3. How strong is it (magnitude)?
4. What structures are involved?
5. What processes occur (cycles, spirals, sequences, turning points)?
6. What are the causes?
7. What are the consequences (and for whom)?
8. What human agency is involved (tasks, strategies)?

Lofland and colleagues do not call their work "grounded theory," but this thinking is based on the Chicago School model and is very consistent with the processes and goals of grounded theory. The first four questions parallel what is done in grounded theory open coding, and the last four questions reflect axial coding in grounded theory.

Another useful resource for techniques to help the researcher move beyond descriptive results to theory building is *Tricks of the Trade* by Howard Becker (1998). Becker, like Strauss, was a student of Blumer and Hughes in sociology at the University of Chicago. This book, subtitled *How to Think about Your Research while Doing It,* is full of ideas and "tricks" designed to stimulate thinking. (For Becker, a "trick" is "a helpful device that helps you solve a problem of thinking.") Some of the terms and processes are identical to those in grounded theory. For example, Becker suggests raising the level of abstraction by focusing on process (action verbs) instead of using descriptive nouns or adjectives. He recommends that you ask questions of your data, such as how actions, interactions, and emotions change over time; look for stages, a process of development, careers, or sequences; and ask whether these changes occur as conditions change.

Memoing in Axial Coding

Memos in the middle stage of grounded theory analysis reflect the ongoing processes of "constant comparison" and "theoretical sampling" that continue throughout grounded theory analysis. Memoing in axial coding involves recording your developing ideas about possible relationships among concepts and categories, as well as your thoughts on the contextual factors, conditions, and consequences relevant to your categories. In memos, you can explore questions about the study, tentative answers, ideas for further sampling, hypotheses, and comparisons of emerging ideas with other theories. Charmaz's (2006) book (see Chapter 3) shows the progression of memos through the various stages of analysis. See Box 4.1 on memos in axial coding.

Axial Coding Furthers the Grounded Theory Process

As I emphasized in Chapter 3 with respect to open coding, axial coding is part and parcel of the grounded theory process. It is not done in

---

Box 4.1 Memos in Axial Coding

- Try to answer the question: "What is going on here?"
- Relate categories to other categories, using their dimensions and properties.
- Use matrices.
- Analyze how people construct actions and processes.
- Identify the context.
- Consider the conditions that affect your categories.
- Consider the consequences of your categories.

isolation, but plays a central role in the development of the theory. The ideas developed in the axial coding process guide the next round of theoretical sampling by clarifying characteristics of those needed in the sample. At this stage of the study, possible relationships, conditions, and consequences developed in the axial coding process are treated as hypotheses to be tested in the next round of data gathering. Some ideas will find support and will move into the developing theory. Others will not be supported and may need to be developed further or possibly dropped. This "testing out" of ideas is used to help identify what will become the "core" category or categories in the next step in coding—selective coding. (See the example provided in Figure 4.7.)

SELECTIVE CODING

In the "selective coding" phase of a grounded theory study, the researcher integrates and refines the theory that has been developed in the open and axial coding stage. This involves identifying a "core" category or categories and then relating the other important categories and concepts to this core category. According to Glaser and Strauss (1967), the core category is a category that appears frequently in the data, is abstract, is related to your other categories, is applicable to other areas, and grows in complexity and explanatory power as you relate it to your other categories.

When the core category is clear, the grounded theory researcher begins to focus the analysis around the core. At this point, coding of other categories emphasizes their relationship to the core category. Further theoretical sampling aims to fill in gaps in the core category and its hypothesized relationships. Selective coding allows the researcher to focus his or her energies and to discontinue open and axial coding for categories and concepts that are not related to the central core. The use of a core category keeps the researcher from being overwhelmed, scattered, or overly broad in focus.

Theoretical Saturation

In grounded theory, one continues to gather data until saturation of the core category or categories is reached. A category is saturated when no new information emerges during coding. That is, no new properties, dimensions, conditions, actions/interactions, or consequences are seen in the data. Glaser and Strauss (1967) insisted on saturation of the core category at a minimum. Saturation of other categories is desirable, but not always necessary.

Identifying a Core Category

Glaser asks students, "What is this a study of?" as a way to help them identify the core category. This is a question that the grounded theory researcher returns to again and again as the study progresses. *Analyzing Social Settings* by Lofland and his colleagues (Lofland et al., 2006) is a helpful resource for selecting a core category. In the section on "focusing data," the authors suggest that the researcher identify the "units," "aspects," and "topics" of the study. This technique helps the researcher to identify what he or she most wants to focus on. Units represent the basic components of the study, and they can be, moving from micro to macro, "practices," "encounters," "roles," "relationships," "groups," "organizations," or "cultures." Aspects can be "emotions," "cognitive processes or meanings," or "hierarchical relationships." By combining the units and aspects of the study, the study topic can be clearly stated. (See Lofland et al. for a valuable table giving examples of qualitative studies that represent the possible "topics.") Identifying the units, aspects, and topics of your study can also help clarify what the study is **not** about. This helps you to focus on what is important in the study and avoid going off on tangents.

Becker's "tricks" can also be used in selective coding (Becker, 1998). For example, Becker describes how his colleague, Bernie Beck, asks students who are in the advanced stage of analysis to answer the question, "What is this research about?" but to answer it without using any of the identifying characteristics of the actual case (p. 126). When I ask my students to do this exercise, they are forced to think more broadly about their study topic. Applying this technique, a study about "social workers" might be described as a study of "professionals who work with people." This exercise helps researchers to broaden their thinking not only about the topic but also about the implications of their findings.

Sometimes the core category is fairly clear early in the study, sometimes it changes throughout the study, and sometimes it remains elusive even at the end of the analysis. This is the way ideas work— you can't force it! In my own work, I can't always identify a single organizing category. It is more important that your analysis reflect your best understanding of what is going on in your data than finding a single category that you identify as "core." Like other components of grounded theory, I encourage you to use a core category if it works for you but not to agonize about it if it doesn't work. It is important not to apply these techniques rigidly. I do recommend trying everything that might work, even if at first it initially seems unlikely to help. Once you have tried out different categories as "core," if you find you are losing important aspects of your analysis, then explain what you did and present your analysis the best way you can. I continue to think about my research, even long after it has been published, and sometimes new, clarifying ideas occur later. Your work will be a valuable addition to the understanding of the substantive area, whether you have a single core category or not. (See exemplars at the end of this chapter.)

Tying the Theory Together

Selective coding involves more than the selection of a core category. At this stage, the researcher needs to review the theory (posited relationships among categories) for completeness, as well as for internal consistency and logic. Additional analysis is needed to tie the components of the theory together, to fill in any remaining gaps, and to test it out in a final round of data gathering (see discussion of "negative case analysis" below). The researcher should be able to explain the central processes of the study, using the concepts in the theory, and their interrelationships.

Diagrams
Diagrams can help grounded theory researchers clarify the connections between the core category and other categories. Since they are often a helpful way to present a complex theory, grounded theory researchers often use diagrams in presenting their results. For example, Figure 4.4 shows how Anderson and Danis (2006) present their results.

In his dissertation, Yan (2002) used a complex diagram to illustrate intercultural conflict (Figure 4.5).

Selective Coding in the Grounded Theory Process

In the later stages of grounded theory analysis, data gathering becomes highly focused. Further data may be sought to saturate the core category.

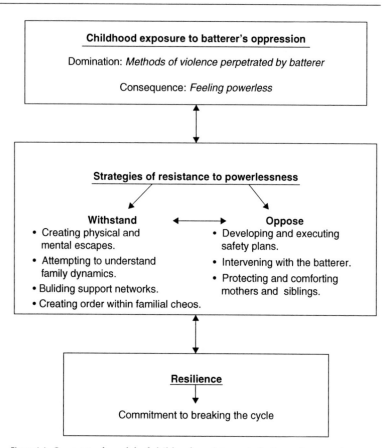

Figure 4.4 Conceptual model of children's resistance to batterers' oppression. Source: Anderson and Danis (2006).

Equally important, the researcher tests out the theory in a final round of data gathering to see whether it holds up and to explore its limits. One way that the grounded theory researcher tests out his or her hypotheses in the later stages of the analysis is to seek out cases that do not fit the hypothesis. This is called "negative case analysis" or "divergent case analysis." To do this type of hypothesis testing, data gathering must continue throughout the research process. Logically, if the researcher is unable to find a case that does not fit the theory, then the theory is more likely to be valid. Of course, not finding a discordant case does not <u>prove</u> the theory, since there is always the possibility that such a case exists

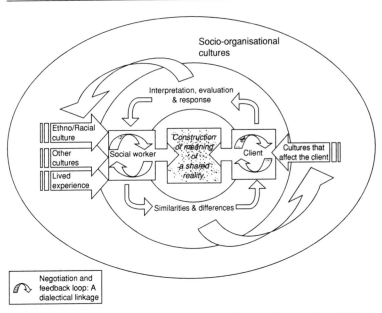

Figure 4.5 A dialectical model of cross-cultural social work. Source: Yan (2002).

(Glaser & Strauss, 1967). The logic behind "negative case analysis" rests on the positivist belief that there is a reality that can be known. When done in other epistemological frameworks, negative case analysis does not have the same meaning. Even so, it can still be a useful technique, because it can help the researcher to fill out his or her theory. For example, when a case is found that does not fit the expected pattern, the researcher can ask, "Under what conditions does this relationship work?" extending the analysis. For example, in my "daughters study," I developed the hypothesis that when their mothers died, daughters were profoundly affected, no matter what their age. In contrast, in cases where mothers survived, daughters returned quickly to normal and did not report a long-term impact of mothers' breast cancer. At the end of my analysis, I looked for new cases that did not fit this pattern. I did not find any women whose mothers died who were not profoundly impacted, but I did find a few women whose mothers survived who did not return to normal. I then used those cases to explore under what conditions the pattern did not hold. For example, in one case, the father left the mother during her illness and the daughter became her mother's caregiver.

After her recovery, the daughter continued to feel responsible for her mother's health and did not want to move on in her own development. The process of looking for "negative cases" helped me to fill in my theory and understand conditions when it did and did not apply. (See further discussion of "negative case analysis" in Chapter 5.)

Techniques to Stimulate Creative, Abstract Thinking

Glaser and Strauss point out that you need ample time to explore the data and allow ideas to emerge. You need to take time to reflect "or you risk collecting large masses of data of dubious theoretical relevance" (Glaser & Strauss, 1967, p. 72). Data analysis is a creative process, and creativity cannot be generated "on demand." This can be frustrating for those who need to develop a schedule for the grounded theory project and ask how much time the data analysis will take. The problem is that creative thinking cannot be done on a schedule, and when you try to do this, it tends to make those creative sparks even less likely, because you are too stressed (see Glaser, 1978).

The specific techniques you employ are less important than the goal: theory development. Sometimes researchers get too obsessed with going through the "correct" steps and forget the reason they wanted to do the research in the first place. If you find that trying one set of techniques is leading you in circles or is boring you, then let that go and try another technique. The point of all of the techniques discussed in this and the last chapter is to stimulate your thinking—to get you to "think outside the box" to use a current cliché—freeing you from the ideas you came in with.

To be truly creative in this work, you need to cultivate a sense of fun and maintain excitement in your work. Locke (2007) defines this as the need to allow the brain to conduct "irrational free-play." Many scientific discoveries occur by serendipity. You need to give yourself the time and the space to allow your mind to move back and forth between rational and playful thinking. This is much harder than simply finding support in your data for preexisting ideas and theories. To create something truly new—a different way of thinking—is difficult, but it can be extremely rewarding! I find that when I want to think creatively, I have to get away from the project and do other things. While I am taking a walk (in nature if possible), listening to music, or even sleeping, I am more likely to get new ideas than when I am sitting at my desk. When I get away, my brain seems to continue working on the analysis, but it is freed up to think in a different way.

I also find that exposing myself to ideas from other fields can spark new ideas. For example, models from physics or biology can sometimes be applied to my field productively. I once attended a medical lecture on an experiment where some body part was removed from a mouse to discover its functions. I found myself thinking that there was a parallel to the motherless daughters in my study. Thinking along these lines, I focused on the importance of mothers in daughters' lives, long past childhood. (See Burstein and Anderson 2011 for a recent discussion of the science of creativity.)

It can be productive to think broadly when looking for comparative examples relevant to your topic. As Glaser said, ". . .treat all as data. . ." (Glaser, 1978, p. 8). Remember to bring your "theoretical sensitivity" to your analysis, considering periodically what your personal experience, professional experience, literature, and theories have to say considering your developing theory.

MEMOS IN ADVANCED STAGES OF ANALYSIS

Even in the advanced stages of grounded theory analysis, memo writing can be very helpful. Box 4.2 shows some appropriate topics for advanced-stage memos. In the late stages of the study, the memos explicate the theoretical model. At this stage, they come closer and closer to the study findings. Memos can later be shaped into publication formats appropriate to the research. In memos, you can explore your ideas in as much detail as you like. Computer software programs (see Chapter 6) can help you to link memos to data that you may want to use to support your conclusions.

PUTTING IT ALL TOGETHER

Coding in grounded theory is not performed in isolation from data gathering, since it is always done to further the constant comparative analysis

---

Box 4.2 Memos in Later Data Analysis

- Consider the question, "What is this a study of?"
- Discuss your core category and how other categories relate to it.
- Identify gaps, categories that are incomplete.
- Explicate ideas, events, actions, or processes.
- Consider conditions related to actions, interactions, and emotions.
- Consider consequences of actions, interactions, and emotions.
- Use diagrams to integrate your theory.
- Use social science framing.
- Move from micro to macro levels of analysis.
- Explore "negative case analysis."

---

and to guide the next round of theoretical sampling. Throughout the coding process, the researcher continues to ask questions of the data and to make comparisons between cases or incidents. In early phases of analysis, the goal of data gathering, coding, and theoretical sampling is to generate concepts. Later in the study, the goal shifts to verifying concepts and their relationships to each other. Also, the concepts become more and more abstract. Charmaz (Figure 4.6) illustrates the grounded theory process, starting with initial data gathering and continuing through the different levels of coding. (Note that Charmaz uses the terms "initial coding" for what I call "open coding," and "focused coding" for what I call "axial coding" and "selective coding.")

Figures 4.7 and 4.8 provide an example of the process of a grounded theory analysis based on the dissertation of Eunice Park Lee (2005). Park Lee studied older Korean immigrants to gain an understanding of their idea of the "good life." (See Chapter 2 for an introduction to this study.) Figure 4.7 shows the activities she completed in each of three rounds of data gathering and analysis. Appendix 4.1 shows the development of her grounded theory through this multistage process from theory generation to theory testing. For each round, Park Lee developed concepts and categories. She then developed possible relationships among the categories' "working hypotheses." On the basis of these, she developed some questions, and these questions were used to guide her next round of data gathering (theoretical sampling). By the end of her study, she had two core categories that integrate her earlier concepts and categories: "continuing self" and "living in harmony with others."

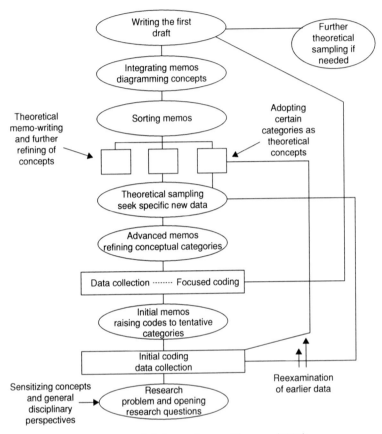

Figure 4.6 Invitation to grounded theory. Source: Charmaz (2006).

THE GROUNDED THEORY PROCESS IN THE EXEMPLAR
SOCIAL WORK STUDIES

Exemplar #1

In her exemplar article, Alaggia (2002) describes her data analysis as follows:

> In the tradition of theoretical sampling, data collection and analysis proceeded simultaneously. Open (a priori) axial, selective coding, and constant comparison of the data (Strauss & Corbin, 1990) was applied

Round I
Develop first interview guide from research questions
First-round data collected **(interview; field notes)**
Data management & analysis
- Transcribe interviews
- Code major categories that emerged
- Write themes about patterns and relationships
- Develop working hypotheses about categories and themes
- Plan next interview guide

Round II
Second-round data collected **(interview; field notes)**
Data management & analysis
- Transcribe interviews
- Code data for new categories and themes
- Collapse and explode categories and themes
- Look for negative cases; reframe or discard outliers
- Identify new themes
- Negotiate themes (i.e., combined and/or ordered new themes with those from first round)
- Refine working hypotheses
- Plan next interview guide

Round III
Third-round data collected **(interview, field notes)**
Data management & analysis
- Transcribe interviews
- Code data for new categories and themes
- Identify major categories reaching saturation
- Collapse and explode categories and themes
- Look for negative cases; Reframe or discard outliers
- Check for categories from all three rounds for saturation and mutual exclusivity
- Negotiate themes (i.e., combined and/or ordered new themes with those from previous interviews)
- Refine working hypotheses
- Negotiate final working hypotheses to develop grounded theory

Figure 4.7 Flow chart of a grounded theory dissertation. Adapted from Park Lee (2005).

for interpretation of the data and assisted by the computerized program. A number of themes, or concepts, evolved as coding was being conducted on the interview data and as analysis proceeded additional participants were interviewed, while new codes were developed when additional underlying factors contributing to mothers' responses became apparent. In relation to support, the following broad categories were developed during the preliminary stages of analysis: 1) belief; 2) affective response and; 3) behavior response. However, as analysis proceeded dimensions of these categories emerged and were further elaborated as supported by the participant responses. Detailed dimensions of these categories, with examples of qualitative quotes evolved as follows. . . . (p. 46)

Exemplar #2

Here is how Anderson and Danis (2006) describe their analytic process:

> Through coding, the data were grouped into final categories that represented key psychosocial issues and patterns (resistance to oppression) that were analyzed by comparing them with one another, so relevant themes (e.g. withstanding and opposing a sense of powerlessness) that addressed the research questions could emerge. Finally, a theory of resilience was generated around the core category that described the central phenomenon related to the participants' experiences. (p. 423)

They went on to say that the core category,

> 'children's exposure to the batterers' oppression' was the central phenomenon that emerged from the data and provided a context for the adversity (abuse and violence) that the participants had experienced. A theory of resilience was generated around this core category to describe and explain the nature and workings of the dominant psychosocial processes within the conceptual model. Specifically, resilience emanated from the participants' acts of resistance that began as spontaneous reactions to their childhood adversity and its consequences and evolved into strategies that the participants used throughout their lives. The conceptual model highlights the interplay between risk (powerlessness) and protective (withstanding and opposing) factors that developed in response to such adversity. For this population, then, resilience involved a process that was promoted by strategies of resistance that the participants drew on throughout their lives and contributed to their commitment to break the cycle of violence. (pp. 424–425)

The authors go on to describe a number of "withstanding" and "opposing" strategies used by the respondents. Finally, the theory is applied to social work practice in the section titled "Discussion and Implications": "Viewing survival strategies as resistance to oppression is consistent with both the feminist empowerment and the strengths perspectives in social work practice. . . . Thus definitions of resilience should be broadened to include the concept of resistance" (p. 429). The authors use the theory to draw implications for helping professionals who work with adult daughters of battered women.

Exemplar #3

In his published studies (Yan, 2008a, 2008b), when Yan describes his methodology, he does not use the terms "open," "axial," or "selective coding." He focuses instead on the "constant comparative method":

> The constant comparison method was used to analyze the data from coding, pattern development and theory building in this study. Constant comparison is more than just an analysis strategy. It is also the essence of the grounded theory approach, through which diversity—similarities and differences—are sorted into categories and dimensions (Glaser & Strauss, 1967). In this study, because of the programmed variations in sampling focus, comparisons were made not only between different interviews, but also between data collected in different stages. (pp. 319–320)

In the dissertation itself, Yan (2002) describes how he came to use this model of analysis:

> The researcher had tried the coding procedure proposed by Corbin and Strauss (1990) [sic], which suggests data should be sorted through open coding, axial coding, selective coding, and the use of a conditional matrix. However, the researcher found it hard to fit the data into their preset framework. Specifically, during the process of making connections between categories, the axial coding was too rigid to dimensionalize and describe the categories of how the participants negotiate with their own cultures. The researcher decided to turn to Glaser's theoretical coding idea (Glaser, 1978), which is less instructive and concrete but more flexible and focuses on emergence. (p. 68)

Yan's open discussion of his process of "trial and error" in selecting his analysis model illustrates how different researchers find different techniques more or less helpful. This is an example of the researcher selecting what works for him, rather than trying to fit his analysis into a model that is too rigid. I find that the more structured analytical methods are often most helpful in the early stages of a study. Then as the analysis takes shape, the researcher feels confident to deviate from the prescribed model.

CHAPTER SUMMARY

This chapter showed how to build theory from the concepts and categories developed in open coding (Chapter 3). I discussed axial coding and selective coding, illustrating these with examples. I showed how matrices and diagrams can be used to further this type of coding. I presented some techniques to stimulate creative thinking in the later stages of coding. I emphasized how these techniques fit into the multistage abductive process of grounded theory analysis. I illustrated the use of these techniques in a dissertation and in the exemplar grounded theory social work studies.

SUGGESTED EXERCISES

1. Try out some of the middle-level coding techniques using your own data. Begin with two or three segments of data that have already been "open coded" and a list of codes and categories you have identified as important to your research question. Identify two or three categories to work on for this exercise, showing the data (text of interview or field note) that support these codes. For each of your categories, please try out several techniques designed to move your categories toward theory, such as:
   • Identifying dimensions and properties of your concepts
   • Considering conditions and consequences
   • Asking theoretical questions
   • Using symbolic interactionism concepts to guide your coding (i.e., code for actions the respondent is taking, look for interactions, meanings, expectations, roles, strategies)
   • Considering the questions "What's going on here?" and "What is your study about?"

- Considering how these codes and categories might relate to each other
2. For your categories, try out several techniques designed to move your categories toward theory, such as:
   - Selective coding: Identifying a central or core category that can be used to organize or integrate the other categories and concepts
   - Developing a "data display," such as a matrix or a diagram (a la Miles and Huberman), to develop the relationships among your concepts
   - Focusing your data, using the concepts and questions from Lofland and colleagues, including social science framing
   - Using Becker's "tricks" to stimulate your thinking, and then memoing about it
3. Write a brief memo on your experience doing the analysis exercise. Was it valuable? What techniques worked well for you? What didn't work? What problems did you have? What might be important "next steps" for your project?

Round 1 (Mrs. I, Mr. H, Mrs. S, Mrs. J, Mrs. P)

A. Categories/Concepts

Objective life conditions
1. Functioning on one's own even with certain health conditions
2. No cognitive impairment
3. Adequate, stable/regular income
4. Living separately from one's children/ being able to sleep comfortably
5. Some proficiency in English
6. Getting around on one's own
7. Well-being of children and grandchildren

"The Good Life"
1. Being healthy—both physically and mentally
2. Being able to enjoy oneself—not engaging in physically demanding work
3. Being able to take care of oneself and provide for one's needs and wishes without being a burden to others
   a. Offspring are doing well, living happily
   b. Being able to do what one wants
      i. Hobby
      ii. Daily living tasks
      iii. Wishes/dreams

Reference group
1. People who are worse off than they are
2. Before and after immigration to the U.S.

Belief
1. "Have to be satisfied"
2. "The wind never stops blowing in a tree with many branches"

B. Working Hypotheses

1. Objective life conditions are considered necessary for "the good life." These life conditions are important because they enable the elderly to take care of themselves and avoid becoming a burden to others, their grown children in particular.

2. When asked to define "the good life," the informants refer to it as happy life and/or satisfying life. "The good life" = happy/satisfying life?

Appendix 4.1 Example of the theory-building process in a grounded theory dissertation. Source: Park-Lee (2005).

3. In addition to providing me a list of life conditions that they believe essential for "the good life," the informants wish to do the following and believe that they are leading a good life if they can realize the following:

4. Reference group/comparison standards are used to evaluate their well-being in old age. The reference group the elderly individuals use place their life circumstances in a positive light.

5. "Have to be satisfied"—When I ask the informants whether they are satisfied with their lives, they tend to tell me "they are satisfied with their lives because they have to be satisfied." In other words, in effect, they are not satisfied with their lives. But because of the following reasons, they force themselves to become content with their lives.
   a. "Otherwise, it is simply being greedy."
   b. Should not ask for more resources to be used on the elderly; taking resources away from their offspring

6. Being able to accept the inevitable
   1. They cannot be of much help to their children.
   2. "The wind never stops blowing in a tree with many branches." Their children's problems are simply a part of life.

C. Questions (incorporated in the interview guide and guided informant selection during the Round 2 data collection)

1. Why are the elderly most concerned about being a burden to their offspring? Why being a burden to their offspring has detrimental effects on the older adults' sense of well-being?

2. Are "the good life," happy life, and satisfying life the same?

3. How are these (e.g., being healthy, enjoying oneself, providing for one's needs without depending on one's offspring) related to "the good life"? Why are they important and necessary for "the good life"?

4. The informants refer to their belief such as "have to be satisfied; otherwise it is simply being greedy" in order to help themselves accept their present life circumstances. In other words, they believe that their present life is less than perfect/ideal. Then, what do they consider an ideal life in old age? What kind of life do they consider truly satisfying that they don't *have to* be satisfied?

5. All of the 5 informants in this round live in a subsidized apartment for seniors. Their monthly income was less than $1,000. I wonder whether individuals who have different life circumstances (e.g., more or less financially comfortable/stable, **owns a home, lives with one's grown children**) have different ideas about "the good life."

6. I had only 1 male informant in this round. I wonder whether there is **gender** differences in the way people define "the good life." I wonder whether married couples with the same/similar life circumstances evaluate their lives in a different manner.

7. All the informants were in their 70s. I wonder whether people who are in **their 80s or 90s** define "the good life" differently.

8. All the informants scored 5 or less on the GDS-SF. I wonder whether individuals with **higher GDS-SF scores** on the measure have different ideas about "the good life" and evaluate their life circumstances differently.

Appendix 4.1 (Continued)

Round 2 (Mr. L, Mrs. L, Mr. S, Mrs. H, Mr. K)

A. Categories/Concepts Reaching Saturation
Objective life conditions

B. New or Further Developed Categories/Concepts
"The Good Life"
1. Physical comfort

a. Health
    i. Functioning on one's own even with certain health conditions
    ii. Cognitively intact

b. Providing for basic needs
    i. Adequate, stable/regular income
    ii. Some English proficiency
    iii. Getting around
        1. Drive
        2. Use public transportation

c. Providing for other physical needs
    i. Enjoying oneself
        1. Pursuing one's hobby
        2. Engaging in other social/leisure activities

d. Physical space
    i. Be able to live and sleep comfortably
    ii. Live separately from one's children
    iii. Live with one's married children but have separate life/daily schedule from that of the offspring

2. Emotional comfort
    a. Having no worries about being a burden to others
        i. Being able to take care of oneself (e.g., daily living tasks)
        ii. Being able to do what one wants without relying on others

    b. Having no worries about offspring: well-being of offspring
        i. Children
            1. Healthy
            2. Make a good living/financially stable
            3. Married and live happily

Appendix 4.1 (Continued)

        ii. Grandchildren
            1. Healthy
            2. Doing well at school
    c. Social/emotional support
        i. Friends
        ii. Offspring

        Strategies:
            1. Not to get involved in their offspring's affair
                a. Accepting that their children have also
                   grown and are adults
                b. Praying for their children
                c. Living separately from the grown children
                d. Not providing unsolicited advice

            2. Learning English

            3. Making oneself busy
                a. Taking English classes
                b. Attending senior center program
                c. Creating activities/programs in which one
                   can participate (e.g., volunteer program)

            4. Seeking different ways to maintain one's health

            5. "Have to be satisfied"

            6. Reference group/comparison standard
                a. People who are worse off than they are
                    i. Other older Korean adults in the U.S.
                    ii. Other older adults in the U.S.
                    iii. Other older adults in Korea

                b. Before and after a critical life event
                    i. Immigration to the U.S.

                c. Hypothetical situation ("If I had never left
                   Korea…)

C. Working Hypotheses

1. "The good life" is different from subjective well-being. "The good life" is an ideal life that the elderly aspire to lead, while subjective well-being is one's perception/evaluation of his or her life.

7. The ideal life, to the informants, implies being able to be the person they have always been (e.g., self-reliant person who does not cause others inconvenience, brave, faithful Christian, parent) without being limited or constrained by changes associated with aging and immigration.

Appendix 4.1 (Continued)

8. How one defines oneself (whether the person sees oneself as an independent entity or in relation to others) influences how one defines "the good life." For instance, to an individual who sees him/her as a self-reliant person, "the good life" means being able to continue being a self-reliant person in old age.

    a. Gender itself does not necessarily seem to cause individuals to define "the good life" in a different manner.

    b. Various experiences that one had over the course of his or her life and what kind of meaning that the individual draws from these experiences influence how one defines the self and "the good life" rather than specific demographics/socioeconomic status of the person (e.g., gender, work status).

9. Objective life conditions are important for "the good life."

    a. Depending on their life circumstances, different individuals consider different conditions more important than others.

    b. Because of their shared experiences as "older immigrants," certain conditions (e.g., English proficiency, getting around freely, not becoming demented) are commonly regarded as essential for "the good life."

10. These life conditions assist the elderly to do what they want/need without relying on their children.

11. The informants say they live a comfortable, good, happy, or satisfying life, indicating the judgment that they have arrived at after evaluating their life circumstances. People arrive at such a judgment about their lives after comparing their actual life with their definition of "the good life."

12. Upon recognizing discrepancies between their actual life and their definition of "the good life," people make efforts to maintain their sense of self and to assist themselves to lead "the good life."

D. Questions

1. Informants that I have interviewed so far report being satisfied with their lives and their scores on the GDS-SF are relatively low. Most of them are in their early to mid-70s. All of them have children and report being satisfied with their relationships with their offspring. I wonder whether similar views on the ideal life in old age will come out of interviews with people:

    • Who are *older* than the informants (e.g., late 70s, in their 80s, 90s)

    • Whose *GDS-SF scores are relatively high* at the time of screening

    • Who are *childless* or *whose relationships with their offspring are unsatisfying*

2. I also wonder whether these individuals will use different strategies in order to protect their sense of self.

Appendix 4.1 (Continued)

Round 3 (Mrs. C, Mrs. J, Mr. H, Mrs. C, Mrs. K)

A. Categories/Concepts Reaching Saturation
Physical comfort
Psychological comfort
Comparison standards

B. New or Further Developed Categories/Concepts
Continuing self
    1. Having the freedom to be the self
        a. Continue being the person one has always been
        b. Being the person one desires to be

    2. Living in harmony with others
        a. Having the freedom to do what one wants
            i. Being physically comfortable = comfort in body
            ii. Being psychologically comfortable = comfort in mind

Efforts/strategies

    1. Behavioral
        a. Maintaining one's health
            i. Diet
            ii. Exercise
            iii. Seeking information on various health
            maintenance methods

        b. Learning English

        c. Utilizing available resources/services

        d. Preparing for future events (e.g., frailty,
        debilitating/terminal illnesses,death)
            i. Seeking information on advanced
            directives/other end-of-life care
            ii. Making attempts to share their ideas of how
            they want to die with their offspring
            iii. Preparing for death every day
    1. Wearing white clothes when going to bed
    2. Living simply; cleaning closet/kitchen

        e. Creating programs/activities in which one can participate to
        provide oneself meaning in life in old age and/or to spare time

Appendix 4.1 (Continued)

    f. Removing oneself from a situation that can distress oneself
        i. Not providing unsolicited advice; not asking their offspring questions about their business/family before they come and seek their advice/opinions
        ii. Living separately from their children

  2. Cognitive
    a. Religions belief
        i. Christianity: being content and grateful for what is given by God
    b. Cultural belief
        i. Pal-Ja —"I am destined to live the way I have led my life.'
        ii. Nae-Ri-Sa-Rang
            1. Redefining one's parental role from "giver" to "receiver"
        iii. Filial piety
            a. Redefining the meaning of filial piety
            b. Redefining how one's children can practice filial piety
        iv. "No limit to being greedy"
        v. "The wind never stops blowing in a tree with many branches."
    c. Manipulating comparison standards

C. Working Hypotheses

1. "The good life" and subjective well-being (SWB) are not the same construct.
    a. "The good life" = ideal life
    b. SWB = a judgment about one's life quality after comparing one's actual life with one's ideal life

2. An ideal life in old age = continuing self while living in harmony with others

3. Changes associated with aging and immigration frequently hinder the elderly from maintaining their sense of self. They often force them to rely on others, their offspring in particular, and limit their freedom in doing what they want/need. As a result, the older adults feel detached from the self—that is, the person they have always been and the person they desire to be.

4. Subjective well-being is an outcome produced as a result of the individual engaging in a cognitive appraisal and coping process. Elderly people compare their life circumstances with their ideal life. If discrepancies are identified, they make efforts to close the gap between the two. These efforts can be divided into two: behavioral and cognitive.

Appendix 4.1 (Continued)

5. Since aging- and immigration- related changes continue to take place, elderly individuals are required to make continuous efforts to maintain their sense of self and create a positive sense of well-being for oneself.

6. Not all efforts yield positive outcomes. Individuals who emphasize the subjective aspect of the quality of life and believe that happiness is not given by others are effective and successful in creating happiness for themselves and report leading a good life.

D. Questions

1. Due to the nature of the study, I can only explore how elderly people define who they are and see how their past life experiences are in supportive of their present self-definition. Since the elderly reconstruct and interpret their life experiences in order to create coherence in their sense of self, I wonder whether the older adults redefine who they are when their efforts to maintain their sense of self fail. I wonder whether this is the most powerful cognitive coping effort that the elderly use in order to create a positive sense of self. If I were to interview these 15 informants in a year or two, they will view themselves and evaluate their life circumstances in the same manner.

2. Individuals with certain personal characteristics (e.g., hardiness, resilience) seem to affect how they deal with their less than perfect life circumstances. I wonder whether individuals who are not hardy or resilient use different coping strategies and evaluate their well-being in a different manner.

Appendix 4.1 (Continued)

5

Evaluating Quality

This chapter addresses ideas of quality in classic and newer versions of grounded theory. I emphasize that in grounded theory, credibility is related to the application of the grounded theory method, as well as to the theory that is produced and to its applicability to practice. I also explore how the contributions of social work authors on evaluating and enhancing quality in qualitative research can be used in grounded theory studies. The chapter includes illustrations of how quality is addressed in grounded theory social work research. As with the other chapters, it ends with suggested exercises for readers to assess grounded theory studies and to enhance credibility/trustworthiness in their own research.

CRITERIA FOR QUALITY IN QUALITATIVE RESEARCH

The question of quality in qualitative research has long been controversial. This issue has a painful history in qualitative research. Before they were widely accepted as legitimate, qualitative studies were often evaluated by applying the standards for quantitative research, such as hypothesis testing, measurement reliability, and generalizability. Not surprisingly, qualitative research did not meet these (quantitative) standards, since it fails to test hypotheses, its methods are not objective (e.g., no blind or double-blind studies, no standardized measures), and

"Ulrich, that's bad science and you know it!"

Figure 5.1 "Ulrich, that's bad science and you know it!" Source: © Edward Koren/
The New Yorker Collection/www.cartoonbank.com (1995).

its results are not generalizable (e.g., no large random samples) (see
Figure 5.1).

In response, qualitative researchers began to develop their own criteria for evaluation. Initially, these mirrored those used by the dominant
quantitative community. An early set of criteria that paralleled the quantitative criteria of internal validity, external validity (generalizability),
reliability, and objectivity was developed for qualitative research called
"credibility," "transferability," "dependability," and "confirmability"
(Lincoln & Guba, 1985). "Credibility" meant that the research has internal consistency; "transferability" referred to the applicability of the findings to other settings; "dependability" referred to the consistency of the
research methods; and "confirmability" meant that the findings should
represent the situation of the respondents and not the subjective views of
the researcher. While these criteria may have helped to legitimate qualitative studies among quantitatively oriented gatekeepers (e.g., editorial

boards, grant funders), they were not acceptable to many qualitative researchers.

Any definition of "quality" is inherently tied to epistemological assumptions, so a discussion of what constitutes quality quickly raises questions on the nature of reality (ontology) and whether the researcher is "inside" that reality or an objective outsider. Epistemology determines not only what is thought to indicate a quality study and how it can be determined but also whether there is even any single knowable definition of "quality." (See discussion in Chapter 1.) While the set of "parallel" criteria can be applied with some success to qualitative methods that operate from a "postpositive" worldview, they are a poor fit with constructivist and postmodernist research models (Morrow, 2005). If all knowledge is constructed, or co-constructed, then the application of criteria designed to challenge the "subjectivity" of the researcher does not apply. In the constructivist worldview, there is no single "truth" or "reality" out there that is being discovered by the researcher. Since consistency is not expected in this model, techniques such as "member checking" or triangulation are not appropriate. Nor is there a clear consensus as to what constitutes a quality study in constructivist and postmodern research.

A second set of "intrinsic" qualitative criteria was developed by the same authors a few years later (Lincoln & Guba, 1985 based on "authenticity." This was elaborated to include "fairness," "ontological authenticity," "educative authenticity," "catalytic authenticity," and "tactical authenticity." These criteria address the problems created by the application of criteria based on "postpositivist" assumptions to research that does not assume the existence of a knowable reality. Criteria of "authenticity" that require that alternative views be explored and presented and that the respondents be invited in as co-researchers to develop and present their views are preferred.

Further complicating the issue of how to determine quality in qualitative research is the fact that different qualitative methods have different goals. Therefore, a single set of standards for quality may not exist, even for methods with the same epistemological assumptions. For example, in action research, criteria for quality may involve social change, social action, and the extent to which the study results in discourse (Morrow, 2005). Other traditions reject any idea of "criteria for judging quality," because this very concept is rooted in societal inequalities where only the most privileged are in a position to render judgments.

Finally, quality has different aspects, and which aspects are emphasized in the different standards are not always clear. Some standards focus on the issue of bias. For example, Padgett (2008) focuses on types of bias and ways to prevent them. She has compiled a list of activities researchers can build into their studies to reduce different sources of bias. Others emphasize the consistency in the study between the epistemology, the methodology, the results, and the implications (Drisko, 1997). Still others focus on the application of the methodology itself, or the value of the product of the research. Sometimes lists of criteria are developed that combine different aspects of quality in ways that can be confusing.

DEVELOPMENT OF CRITERIA FOR QUALITY IN GROUNDED THEORY RESEARCH

The fact that the goal of grounded theory is to produce theory, standards for quality in grounded theory are somewhat different from those in other qualitative traditions. Since grounded theory provides a fairly explicit methodology, assessments of the quality of grounded theory studies often emphasize the extent to which the researcher adheres to the grounded theory method. In grounded theory studies, the theory that is produced in the study can be assessed. Because of these differences, grounded theory researchers need to develop an understanding of how quality is viewed in the grounded theory tradition. Long before Lincoln and Guba attempted to define and measure quality in qualitative research (1985, 1989), Glaser and Strauss (1967) presented criteria for judging the quality of grounded theory studies. These standards address both the process of the study (how the study was done) and the product of the study (the theory itself).

Criteria Related to Application of the Grounded Theory Method

In *Discovery* (1967), Glaser and Strauss included two chapters dealing with the issue of quality, pointing out that the criteria used to evaluate theory verification studies (quantitative) are not appropriate for studies that aim to generate theory such as grounded theory. In the first of these, titled "The Credibility of Grounded Theory," they recognized that researcher bias could interfere with credibility of the theory produced in the study.

> A sociologist often develops a theory that embodies, without his realizing it, his own ideals and the values of his occupation and social class, as well as popular views and myths, along with his deliberate efforts at making logical deductions from some formal theory to which he became committed as a graduate student. (p. 238)

To Glaser and Strauss, the most important way to enhance credibility was for the researcher to adhere closely to the grounded theory method. They advised careful examination of how data was gathered, who was interviewed, what was observed, what kinds of comparisons were made, and how the researcher came to his or her conclusions. They argued that if the researcher uses the constant comparative technique and carefully saturates his or her concepts and categories, the resulting theory will be credible. They identified several critical techniques that are a part of grounded theory method.

> [The researcher] believes not because of an arbitrary judgment but because he has taken very special pains to discover what he thinks he may know, every step of the way from the beginning of his investigation until its publishable conclusion. . . . A field worker knows that he knows, not only because he has been in the field and because he has carefully discovered and generated hypotheses, but also because "in his bones" he feels the worth of his final analysis. He has been living with partial analyses for many months, testing them every step of the way, until he has built his theory. (p. 225)

Glaser and Strauss trust the theory that results from careful application of grounded theory methods in part because results are based on immersion in a social world. This was a critical component of the Chicago School field studies.

> But a firsthand immersion in a sphere of life and action a -social world-different from one's own yields important dividends. The field worker who has observed closely in this social world has had, in a profound

sense, to live there. He has been sufficiently immersed in this world to know it, and at the same time has retained enough detachment to think theoretically about what he has seen and lived through. (p. 226)

The chapter on credibility also advises grounded theory researchers how to convey to others the credibility of the discovered theory.

. . .describe the data of the social world studied so vividly that the reader, like the researchers, can almost literally see and hear its people-but always in relation to the theory. . . . He can quote directly from inter-views or conversations that he has overheard. He can include dramatic segments of his on-the-spot field notes. (pp. 228–229)

Another strategy discussed by Glaser and Strauss is to search for negative cases, or for alternative hypotheses.

In sum, Glaser and Strauss (1967) argue that the application of the constant comparative method overcomes researcher bias because it requires the researcher to keep track of the development of his or her ideas. They identified the following strategies, built into the grounded theory method, that enhance credibility: (1) immersion in the field, (2) generation and testing of hypotheses in the field (not before the data gathering begins), (3) use of memos to trace the development of ideas, (4) detailed and vivid description to support conclusions, and (5) pursuit of alternative explanations and negative cases.

Criteria Related to the Grounded Theories Themselves

In addition to the careful application of the method itself, grounded theory can also be evaluated on the basis of the quality of the theory pro-duced. For this, Glaser and Strauss (1967) saw the responsibility for ensuring credibility to be shared by the researcher and the reader. "The integration and clarity of the theory will, however, increase the probabil-ity that colleagues will accept its credibility" (p. 230). That is, they sug-gest that the reader consider the study in light of his or her own prior knowledge and experience, and use them to weigh whether the theory seems credible.

The researcher ought to provide sufficiently clear statements of theory and description so that readers can carefully assess the credibility of the theoretical framework he offers. . . . The cardinal rule for readers is that they should demand explicitness about important interpretations. . . . (p. 233)

Of special importance to social workers, Glaser and Strauss emphasized that a good grounded theory should be applicable in the real world. That is, an important criterion for credibility is whether the theory is useful in practice. "The theory can be applied and adjusted to many situations with sufficient exactitude to guide their thinking, understanding and research" (p. 233). This is elaborated in the second chapter on judging quality in grounded theory research, "Applying Grounded Theory." In it, Glaser and Strauss describe four properties that are needed for application of the theory (see Box 5.1). These are (1) fit, (2) understandability by those in the substantive area, (3) the theory must be sufficiently general to apply to a multitude of situations (not overly narrow), and (4) it must allow the user some control over what is happening in the substantive setting. This last property is particularly important for social workers and other professionals who aim to use the theory to intervene in social situations.

Glaser and Strauss argue that when the researcher has "forced" his or her theory, it will not have a good "fit" with the substantive area. The second criterion is that it must be understandable, not to other researchers but to those who practice in the field. "A grounded substantive theory that corresponds closely to the realities of an area will make sense and be understandable to the people working in the substantive area" (p. 239). Glaser and Strauss assumed that grounded theory research would be conducted by sociologists and then applied by professionals such as social workers and nurses. Glaser and Strauss saw the use of the theory by

---

Box 5.1 Criteria for a Grounded Theory to Be of Use in Practice

- Fit
- Be understandable by those in the substantive (practice) area
- Be sufficiently general to apply to a multitude of situations
- Allow the user some control over what is happening in the substantive setting

Source: Glaser and Strauss (1967)

professionals or "laymen" as a way to further enhance the validity of the theory, since they could test it out in their own work.

> Further, these concepts provide a necessary bridge between the theoretical thinking of sociologists and the practical thinking of people concerned with the substantive area, so that both may understand and apply the theory. . . . In particular, these concepts allow this person [practitioner] to pose and test his own favored hypotheses in his initial applications of the theory. Whether the hypotheses are proved somewhat right or wrong, the answers are related to the substantive theory, which helps both in the interpretation of hypotheses and in the development of new applications of the theory. (p. 241)

Glaser and Strauss felt that the theory needed to be applicable to "multi-conditional, ever-changing daily situations. . . . The person who applies the theory will, we believe, be able to bend, adjust or quickly reformulate a grounded theory when applying it, as he tries to keep up with and manage the situational realities that he wishes to improve" (p. 242). In this case, the "person" would be a practitioner, such as a social worker or a nurse. This practitioner is not only someone whose role is to apply the theory, but also a true partner with the grounded theory researcher, who adapts the theory to the practice context. (See Hall & Callery [2001] for a discussion of "relationality" in grounded theory.)

The third criterion for applying grounded theory, "generality" means that the theory can be applied in a variety of situations. This section makes it clear that practitioner application of the theory (and adaptation of it to the setting) is critical to the validation of the theory.

> This diversity facilitates the development of a theory with both a sufficient number of general concepts relevant to most situations and plausible relations among these categories to account for much everyday behavior in the situations. . . . The application is thus, in one sense, the theory's further test and validation. (pp. 243–244)

Clearly, the generators of grounded theory foresaw collaboration between practitioners and researchers. Also of importance to social workers and other practitioners is the final criterion discussed by Glaser and Strauss in the chapter on application: control.

> The substantive theory must enable the person who uses it to have enough control in everyday situations to make its application worth trying. . . . The person who applies the theory must be enabled to understand and analyze ongoing situational realities, to produce and predict change in them, and to predict and control consequences both for the object of change and for other parts of the total situation that will be affected. (p. 245)

To summarize, Glaser and Strauss state:

> A theory with controllable concepts of sufficient generality, that fits and is understandable, gives anyone who wishes to apply these concepts to bring about change a *controllable theoretical foothold* in diverse situations. The controllability of a conceptual variable is enhanced by its being part of a theory that guides its use under most conditions that the user is likely to encounter. (p. 245)

In addition to concepts they can control, Glaser and Strauss value concepts that help practitioners know what conditions are applicable to the theory, what consequences they might expect under certain conditions, and what conditions might determine who has access to those in control. For example, doctors may have control of the conditions of awareness (openness) of information about death in hospitals, but nurses have control through their easy access to the doctors. Thus, ideally, it is important to include the organizational culture in the theory.

In concluding the chapter on the application of grounded theory, Glaser and Strauss refer back to John Dewey and their pragmatist roots.

> Further, as John Dewey has clarified for us, grounded theory is applicable *in* situations as well as *to* them. Thus people in situations for which a grounded theory has been generated can apply it in the natural course of daily events. (pp. 249–250)

In essence, Glaser and Strauss argued that the true test of quality in a grounded theory study is based on how useful the theory is in practice. The proof is in the pudding.

I provided a detailed description of the original criteria developed by Glaser and Strauss (1967). While the criteria developed by Glaser and Strauss on credibility are well known and widely used, those on the applicability of the theory to practice have received far less attention. As a social work researcher, I am excited about their description of a partnership between researcher and practitioner, inductively developing theory, testing it in practice situations, and together modifying the theory as needed. It is this vision of a truly theory-based practice that makes the grounded theory model so promising for the social work field.

More Recent Views of Quality in Grounded Theory

Glaser (1978) provided some elaboration of the criteria he originally developed with Strauss (discussed above) emphasizing "fit," "work," "relevance," and "modifiability." These criteria were further elaborated in Glaser's later work (Glaser, 1998; Stern & Porr, 2011). Strauss and Corbin (1990) also provided further elaboration, focusing on the procedures used by the researchers (see Box 5.2). "Readers are not actually present during the actual analytic sessions, and the monograph does not necessarily help them imagine these sessions or their sequence. . . . The detail must be sufficient to give some reasonable grounds for judging the adequacy of the research process" (Strauss & Corbin, 1998, p. 269).

They also identified nine criteria for a quality grounded theory study that focus on the theory that is produced in the study (see Box 5.3).

Box 5.2 Criteria for Evaluating the Application of the Grounded Theory Method

- How was the original sample selected?
- What major categories emerged?
- What indicators pointed to these categories?
- On the basis of what categories did "theoretical sampling" proceed?
- What were some of the hypotheses pertaining to conceptual relations among categories?
- Were there instances when hypotheses did not explain what was happening in the data?
- How and why was the core category selected?

Source: Strauss & Corbin (1990)

Box 5.3 Criteria for Evaluating the Theory Produced in a Grounded
Theory Study

- Were concepts generated?
- Were the concepts systematically related?
- Do the categories have "conceptual density"?
- Is "variation" built into the theory?
- Do broader conditions explain variation?
- Is "process" taken into account?
- Do the theoretical findings seem significant?
- Does the theory stand the test of time?

Source: Strauss & Corbin (1998)

More recently, Charmaz (2006) considered the evaluation of grounded theory from a constructivist paradigm. She identified four criteria: "credibility," "originality," "resonance," and "usefulness." Consistent with the constructivist views, she does not present these as a single "right" way to evaluate grounded theory studies, but as criteria that "may give you some ideas" (p. 182). "Criteria for evaluating research depend on who forms them and what purposes he or she invokes. . . . We need to consider our audiences, be they teachers or colleagues. They will judge the usefulness of our methods by the quality of our final product" (p. 182).

Finally, in a recent text, Birks and Mills (2011) identify three factors that influence quality in the conduct of grounded theory research: researcher expertise, methodological congruence, and procedural precision. They also discuss the application of grounded theories in practice situations, illustrating the process of moving from the theory to interventions.

SOCIAL WORK PERSPECTIVES ON THE EVALUATION OF QUALITATIVE RESEARCH

While there is no single accepted set of criteria for quality in qualitative research today, social work authors have added helpful perspectives to the broader question of the evaluation of qualitative studies. These are not specific to grounded theory, but they are still important as they are widely used as standards in the social work field. Drisko (1997) focuses primarily on how qualitative studies should be presented, identifying six criteria: 1) identification of the chosen philosophy/epistemology, 2) identification of audience and objectives, 3) specification of the study method, 4) identification of biases, 5) maintenance of social work ethics, and 6) assurance of consistency between conclusions and study philosophy, objectives, and presented data. Applying these to grounded theory, four of these criteria (#1, #2, #3, and #6) require, at a minimum, that the aim of the study should be consistent with grounded theory goals, and that an author who describes his or her methodology as grounded theory should show evidence that he or she actually used grounded theory methods. Since the goal of grounded theory is to develop theory, a study that describes itself as a grounded theory study should have theory development as its aim. Also, its methodology should incorporate the key components of grounded theory. The results should be identifiable in grounded theory terms (e.g., concepts and categories are identified and related to each other).

While grounded theory methods are designed to reduce bias (criteria #4), the explicit statement of bias is not part of the classic grounded theory tradition. Criteria #5, too, is a valuable addition to the grounded theory tradition, which was developed before the emergence of ethical oversight of research (see discussion in Chapter 6).

Drisko's (1997) focus on the importance of consistency between goals and methodology is an especially valuable contribution to social work because, unfortunately, social work researchers do not always meet this standard. This is apparent if we use the scale for rating qualitative studies developed by Sandelowski and Barroso (2003) (see Figure 5.2). The scale ranges from studies with "no findings" to those that provide "interpretive explanations." In a "thematic survey," the researcher identifies common themes, but the themes are not fully described or explained. Instead, like a quantitative study, they are counted and presented as a frequency list. In a "conceptual/thematic description" study, themes are identified and described. Data may be presented to support the theme and to show its dimensions. However, the themes identified are not related to each other, nor are their categories, consequences, dimensions, or conditions developed. Because the themes are simply listed and not related to each other, they do not constitute a fully developed theory.

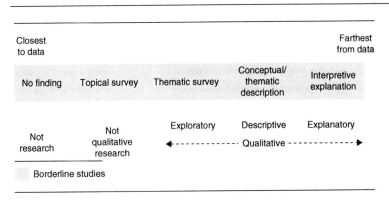

Figure 5.2 Typology of qualitative findings. Source: Sandelowski and Barroso (2003).

Grounded theory falls into the most abstract level, "interpretive explanation" studies, which transform data to

> produce grounded theories, ethnographies or otherwise fully integrated explanations of some phenomenon, event or case. . . . In contrast to findings that survey topics and themes without linking them, or that conceptually or thematically describe elements of experience without explaining them, interpretive explanations offer a coherent model of some phenomenon, or a single thesis or line of argument that addresses causality or essence. Moreover, these explanations fully attend to relevant variations in both sample and data. (p. 914)

Studies that are "thematic surveys" and "conceptual/thematic descriptions" are not appropriately labeled "grounded theory" studies. Recent reviews on studies that described themselves as "grounded theory" in social work literature (O'Connor, Netting, & Thomas, 2008; Oktay, 2006; Wells, 1995) suggest that there is confusion about what constitutes a grounded theory study. Social work researchers with a wide variety of goals claimed to be using grounded theory, when these techniques were not well suited to their aims (O'Connor et al., 2008). Some authors use the term "grounded theory" interchangeably with "qualitative research," as when they justify using grounded theory because little is known about a topic. Some use open coding procedures as a justification for labeling a study "grounded theory." This is not appropriate because open coding is common in many types of qualitative research. In grounded theory, coding is used in conjunction with other techniques such as constant comparison, theoretical sampling, etc., in the context of a multistage process of data gathering alternating with data analysis for the purpose of generating middle-range theories.

A different approach to quality is found in Padgett's text on qualitative research in social work (2008). Focusing primarily on the process of conducting the research, Padgett identifies three sources of bias common in qualitative studies, and develops a generic set of methods that researchers can use to reduce them. The three potential sources of bias are "reactivity," "researcher bias," and "respondent bias." Researcher bias occurs when "observations, and interpretations are clouded by perceptions and personal opinions of the researcher. Emotional pitfalls can also contribute to researcher bias" (Padgett, 2008, p. 184). Reactivity means a bias that results because the presence of the researcher causes a change in the setting or the respondents. An obvious example would be when the study is of an illegal behavior, because the study participants' behavior may be very different when they know they are being observed. "Respondent bias" occurs when respondents themselves misrepresent themselves or their cultures in an attempt to please the researcher (called "social desirability" in quantitative research) or to make themselves look good. For Padgett, each of the "threats to trustworthiness" can be minimized by applying a set of techniques consisting of "prolonged engagement," "triangulation," "peer debriefing/support," "member checking," "negative case analysis," and "audit trail" (see Figure 5.3).

As an exemplar, Padgett presents a study by Morrow and Smith that used all six mechanisms (Morrow & Smith, 1995). Morrow and Smith conducted a grounded theory study of women who had been sexually abused as children. They conducted multiple interviews over a period of 16 months (prolonged engagement). They met weekly with an interdisciplinary research group (peer debriefing and support). They were able to triangulate their data by using interviews, videotapes of focus groups, and documents. They involved the research participants as co-researchers (member checking). Auditing was a part of their methodology by virtue of memos and a record of how their coding scheme developed over time, in addition to a chronological narrative of their activities. Finally, they actively searched for disconfirming evidence (negative case analysis).

Threat to trustworthiness

Strategy	Reactivity	Researcher bias	Respondent bias
Prolonged engagement	+	−	+
Triangulation	+	+	+
Peer debriefing/ support	0	+	0
Member checking	+	+	+
Negative case analysis	0	+	0
Audit trail	0	+	0

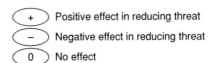

+) Positive effect in reducing threat
−) Negative effect in reducing threat
0) No effect

Figure 5.3 Threats to trustworthiness. Source: Padgett (2008).

Since Padgett's recommendations were developed for all qualitative research and not specifically for grounded theory, it is interesting to compare these mechanisms to enhance validity with those discussed by Glaser and Strauss in *Discovery* (1967). Their focus on "immersion in the field" is similar to Padgett's "prolonged engagement." Glaser and Strauss's emphasis on testing the theory in the field is related to what Padgett calls "member checking." Member checking is also similar to the criteria of "fit" and "understandability." The use of memos in grounded theory is similar to the use of a journal and an "audit trail" in Padgett. Glaser and Strauss talked about vivid descriptions, which is similar to Padgett's "thick description" (2008)—an idea originally developed by Geertz (1973). Finally, searching for negative cases is mentioned by Padgett in an earlier edition of her book (1998b). Padgett's mechanism of "peer debriefing," not mentioned in the classic grounded theory texts, is a valuable addition to grounded theory research in social work.

WHAT'S TODAY'S GROUNDED THEORY RESEARCHER TO DO?

The wide range of criteria and many recommendations and standards in the grounded theory field (not to mention the broader arena of qualitative research) can be overwhelming. It may be helpful to think of these standards as important goals, and not to let yourself get discouraged if they are not always reachable. Some are more relevant to some types of studies than others, and some are more useful when you are designing a study, while others are of more value when you are evaluating a completed piece of work. Some of the goals for grounded theory cannot be known until the theory is applied in the field, which might be many years after it is published.

It is important to begin thinking about quality criteria at the beginning—not at the end—of a study. Chapter 2, in which I discussed the appropriate aims and conditions for grounded theory research, is very relevant to the issues raised in this chapter on assessing quality. This discussion included both the application of the methodology (as is discussed in detail in grounded theory texts), but equally important, I emphasized that the aim of grounded theory is theory development and discussed the selection of an appropriate research problem and the temperament of the researcher. When you are designing a study, it is important to pay attention to the criteria for quality related to the careful application of the method. Equally important is careful consideration of the goal of the study, the extent to which the research question and method are consistent with the proposed research and the fit between researcher characteristics (theoretical sensitivity and temperament) and the proposed study. The theoretical sensitivity that a particular researcher brings to the problem is another important component of a quality grounded theory study. Often, potentially poor-quality studies can be reshaped into good ones at the beginning by anticipating potential problems. As discussed in Chapter 2, bias can be reduced even before a study has begun by taking potential bias into consideration when selecting a topic. It is often possible to shift the focus of the topic, or the method, to reduce bias in a study. (See discussion in Chapter 2.)

Today's grounded theory researcher should consider both the early recommendations of the founders of the grounded theory method as well as the more recent recommendations, consistent with the development of both grounded theory and qualitative research in general. The classic criteria relating to the way the study was done and to the quality of the theory that was produced by the study are both important.

The mechanisms used need to reflect the study, whether they are part of the grounded theory tradition or not. In addition to the techniques mentioned by Glaser and Strauss, grounded theory researchers can sometimes strengthen their studies by adopting methods that developed in other qualitative methods. However, whatever techniques you use should fit the rationale and the philosophical assumptions of your study. As a pragmatist, I use whatever techniques I find valuable for a particular study. When considering criteria related to how the study will be/was done, there can be a tendency for researchers to focus too much on techniques without giving enough thought to the sources of bias most likely to affect the particular study in question. A study with six techniques is not necessarily a better-quality study than one with five or four. Credibility or trustworthiness depends not just on how many techniques were used, but also on how they were implemented and, more important, with consideration of what threats are most pertinent to the study.

If it is appropriate, I use peer debriefing and try to include debriefers from different fields and/or perspectives. Involving social workers is valuable if you want your theory to be used in practice. Some constructivist models require the researcher to do self-exploration throughout the study. Some authors (Hall & Callery, 2001) recommend that grounded theory researchers incorporate reflexivity into their studies. Mruck and Mey (2007) illustrate how reflexivity is relevant to every phase of a grounded theory study. I use a reflexive journal in all of my own research and find it extremely helpful. "Relationality" is a concept that comes from participatory action research (Hall & Callery, 2001). I find that adding a community advisory board to the study can be a very valuable component, especially if the study will have practical applications for the community. Community advisors can not only help with interpretation of unexpected results and ask questions you may not have thought of but also help with study implications and dissemination of results.

Even when you have done your best to conduct a quality grounded theory study, you can't be sure that the theory produced will meet the criteria of "fit" and "understandable" and "relevant." Nor can you know at the time whether your theory will be applicable and will make a valuable contribution to the field. I often get valuable feedback when I am presenting my results at conferences. For example, when I present posters on the results of the "daughters study," a variety of people come by and comment on the results. But there are always a few who walk up and suddenly stop and examine the poster closely, staring at the quotes, reading every word, and sometimes tearing up. These are almost always daughters themselves. Sometimes we talk, but other times I just let them relate to the study. Words are not necessary. I can see and feel their response. When this happens, I know that I have found something that is true.

Because grounded theory studies result in theories, the evaluation of grounded theory includes evaluation of the theory produced, and not just how the method was applied. Grounded theory studies should discuss the implications of the study findings for the practice field. I am satisfied with the quality of my work when practitioners who work with the population I studied find my findings consistent with their experience and can see how they can use the theory in practice. In my book on the daughters of women with breast cancer (Oktay, 2005), I developed a list of practice implications that I developed directly from the theory. For example, one of the findings was that communication was difficult in these families, so I included a discussion of things that social workers can do to improve communication. Because age and phase of illness were critical categories in my analysis, I targeted my recommendations to specific age and phase categories. Speaking to practitioners who work with families with children, I wrote, "Families with younger daughters were especially likely to need help with communication about the disease, since communication tended to be more open in families with older daughters. Women who have breast cancer need to learn how to share information with their families, especially children and young adolescents, without frightening them" (p. 314).

ILLUSTRATION IN SOCIAL WORK EXEMPLARS

I selected the three exemplar studies precisely because I think they meet the important standards for quality grounded theory studies in social work. Each exemplar study aimed to develop theory, focused on a problem that could be studied using the person-environment focus (symbolic interactionism), brought strong theoretical sensitivity to the study while avoiding bias, applied the key components of the grounded theory method, was strengthened with mechanisms to reduce the impact of bias, developed theory (i.e., dense concepts and categories and the relationships between them), and drew implications from the theory for practice. Many of these characteristics have been discussed in the previous chapters. Here, I call attention to the use of mechanisms to enhance credibility, and application of the theory to practice.

Exemplar # 1

Alaggia (2002) writes in her method section, "Establishing trustworthiness in qualitative research ensures credibility, confirmability, dependability and transferability. Measures for ensuring trustworthiness such as prolonged engagement, persistent observation, member checking and peer review were adhered to" (p. 43). She goes on to describe how she established rapport with her respondents through recruitment, a two- to three-hour interview, and a follow-up call. She used "key experts" (peer debriefing) to explore alternative hypotheses (negative case analysis). Member checking was incorporated through the identification of three of the respondents, who discussed and elaborated the researcher's explanations. In terms of the theory's application, Alaggia includes a section in her article on "implications for assessment and treatment."

> Using a systematic framework of assessment may help to determine strengths better, areas of concern, and avenues of intervention. With mothers who are supportive to the abused child, clinicians need to clearly identify and reinforce supportive responses. In cases where mothers are less supportive, clinicians need to determine the source of difficulties in order to foster more supportive responses. Within the emotionally charged circumstances mothers are faced with after discovery/disclosure of intra-familial sexual abuse the framework shown in Table I is

offered as a tool for assessing the complexities of maternal response, and changes over time, therefore allowing for specific targeting for areas of intervention. (p. 52)

Exemplar #2

In their study of adult daughters of battered women, Anderson and Danis (2006) relied on member checking and peer debriefing to enhance trustworthiness in their study. Participants were given written and oral summaries of their responses and a variety of opportunities to correct them. They also used "ongoing consultations" with colleagues external to the study to process their impressions and "maintain objectivity" (p. 423). They apply their results to clinicians in this quotation:

> For helping professionals who work with the adult daughters of battered women, it is also important to help women recognize how their strategies of resistance led to their resilience. By recognizing the oppressive environment that was created by the batterers' abuse and the various ways in which they personally challenged that oppression, women may be able to transcend interpersonal notions of violence and develop a more comprehensive understanding within a feminist framework. (p. 430)

Exemplar #3

Yan's 2008 papers focus most heavily on the application of the grounded theory method to ensure credibility. He does not explicitly discuss specific mechanisms to enhance credibility in these papers, but his dissertation (2002) includes an extensive discussion of the issues of trustworthiness and fit, where he stresses his use of "thick description": "In this study, the thick description is the principle behind the writing of the findings and discussion chapters. Data from the transcripts are quoted extensively to reflect participants' perspectives" (p. 74). He also used an audit trail and triangulation. Yan also discusses how social work practitioners can apply his theory.

> To be culturally sensitive, social workers should extend their cultural assessment from individual—both their clients' and their own—cultures

to socio-organizational cultures. Instead of focusing only on how individuals' cultures may affect the cause of the problem and the coping capability of the individuals, we should better articulate how other cultures, including those of our organizations and of the society at large, may influence our clients, as well as how various forms of cultural tension may affect our intervention process. (p. 327)

Chapter Summary

In this chapter, I discussed some of the factors that make determining clear criteria for quality in grounded theory difficult. I reviewed the original work of Glaser and Strauss (1967) on credibility and applicability of grounded theory, and discussed how more recent authors have addressed this issue. I emphasized the importance of grounded theory's focus on evaluating the theory itself to social work, especially its usefulness to practitioners. To this discussion, I added a discussion of contributions of social work authors who have discussed the evaluation of qualitative studies and discussed specific mechanisms to enhance the credibility/ trustworthiness of the study, and I showed how these relate to the grounded theory model. I used my own research and the exemplar social work studies to illustrate how these criteria are used in grounded theory social work research.

SUGGESTED EXERCISES

1. Using Glaser and Strauss's criteria for evaluating grounded theory studies according to the way the grounded theory method was applied, evaluate each of the exemplar studies.
2. Using Glaser and Strauss's criteria for a theory that would be applicable to practice, evaluate each of the exemplar studies. Do you think these studies can be of use to social work practitioners? How?
3. For each of the three exemplar studies, identify what you see to be the potential threats to trustworthiness. Is there a basis to suspect researcher bias, reactivity, and/or respondent bias? For example, Alaggia has many years of experience working in a clinical capacity with the respondent population. Do you think this

creates a potential for bias? What techniques did she use to reduce this bias? Were there other things these researchers could have done to increase the trustworthiness of their studies?

4. Considering your own research, which of the three types of bias would be likely to compromise the trustworthiness of your research project? What mechanisms could you build in to counter these?

5. Grounded theory researchers need to respond to "gatekeepers" (editorial boards, grant funders) who do not have a good understanding of the grounded theory method or even of qualitative methods. Consider how would you respond to a reviewer who asks what you consider to be inappropriate questions about your research, such as, "How can you generalize from such a small sample?"

6

Grounded Theory in Social Work Research: Problems and Promise

Chapter 6 addresses how grounded theory is affected by a variety of recent developments in social work research. These include a discussion of why it is sometimes difficult to conduct a grounded theory study today, and what to do when you want to develop theory but it is impractical to apply the grounded theory method as it has been described in the previous chapters of this volume. The chapter also considers ethical and IRB issues in grounded theory research. Attention is given to the practical considerations of publishing formats for grounded theory studies, with illustrations from exemplar grounded theory studies. I also discuss the use of computer software programs in grounded theory analysis. I consider the use of grounded theory in mixed method research. Finally, I discuss "formal grounded theory," the grounded theory model for synthesizing qualitative studies. Exercises designed to help readers apply the material in the chapter to their own research are provided.

DOING GROUNDED THEORY IN TODAY'S RESEARCH ENVIRONMENT

In the previous chapters, I have described grounded theory using the models developed by Glaser and Strauss (1967), Strauss and Corbin

(1990, 1998), Corbin and Strauss (2008), and, to some extent, Charmaz (2006). It has been over 40 years since the original publication (Glaser & Strauss, 1967), and even more since the research it was based on was conducted. Glaser and Strauss provide the following description of their data-gathering process in *Time for Dying*:

> . . .the reader who is unacquainted with this style of research need only imagine the sociologist moving rather freely within each medical service, having announced to the personnel his intention of "studying terminal patients and what happens around them." He trails personnel around the service, watching them at work, sometimes questioning them about details. He sits at the nursing station. He listens to conversations. Occasionally he queries the staff members, either about events he has seen or about events someone has described to him. Sometimes he interviews personnel at considerable length, announcing "an interview," perhaps even using a tape recorder. He sits in on staff meetings. He follows, day by day, the progress of various patients, observing staff interaction with them and conversation with them. He talks with patients, telling them only that he is "studying the hospital." His field work takes place during the day, evening and night; it may last from ten minutes to many hours. (Glaser & Strauss, 1968, p. xi)

The research Glaser and Strauss did on dying took place over many years, during which the researchers conducted observations on the wards of six hospitals, and they later observed 10 additional hospitals in Europe. The results were published in three books—in addition to the book on the grounded theory method. As Glaser and Strauss became aware of different aspects of dying (e.g., slow or fast, expected or unexpected), they were able to move to different settings (theoretical sampling) where they were able to "compare and contrast" (constant comparison) to expand their theory. They had the time needed to continue the research until they achieved "theoretical saturation." The research environment has changed considerably since that time. At the time that Glaser and Strauss developed the model, social science researchers did not have to satisfy IRBs, so they were able to suggest (in the 1967 book) that the literature review and theoretical framework be postponed until after the grounded theory emerged from the data. It is hard to imagine a study like this being done today. It was under these conditions that the key components of grounded theory discussed in earlier chapters developed. Today's researcher may only dream of such free-ranging access to data, seemingly without time limitations and other constraints.

Grounded theory researchers today must obtain the permission of various "gatekeepers" such as IRBs, grant funders, dissertation committees, and possibly others before they can begin data gathering. These gatekeepers often do not understand grounded theory and review all proposals by applying the principles of quantitative research, where literature reviews and clear theoretical frameworks are essential criteria for a quality study. This conflicts with the grounded theory model, where the research question comes out of the data, through the constant comparative process, as do the concepts, categories, conditions, and consequences. The use of theoretical sampling in grounded theory means that these are simply not known in advance.

Theoretical saturation is another characteristic of grounded theory that often creates difficulties for today's researchers. Whether a doctoral student, a faculty member on a sabbatical, or a grant seeker, today's researcher is expected to know in advance how many cases will be in the study and how long the research will take. In grounded theory, the time that the study will take cannot be predicted with accuracy. Since data collection, coding, and analysis are done simultaneously, and since the nature of the data that will be needed to saturate the theoretical concepts is not known in advance, it is virtually impossible to predict the length of the study.

In addition to the difficulty predicting how long it will take, today's researcher may not have the luxury of continuing the study to saturation. As Glaser and Strauss point out, the analytic process requires ample time to explore the data, or "you risk collecting large masses of data of dubious theoretical relevance" (Glaser & Strauss, 1967, p. 72). This may be difficult to explain to those who lack an understanding of the grounded theory method. It also makes anyone using the research to further an end (such as a grant-funded study or a doctoral dissertation) uncomfortable. No one wants to begin a study that could go on for years as they seek "theoretical saturation."

Limited Grounded Theory Studies

The grounded theory method as I have presented it can be thought of as an ideal—something to strive for but, at the same time, something that cannot easily be achieved in today's research climate. For the reasons discussed above, researchers today may have difficulty incorporating all of the key components of the grounded theory model. However, if the goal of the study is the development of new theory, the researcher may be able to do a study that approximates the grounded theory model. Similar to the way a "quasi-experimental" design is used in quantitative research (Cook & Campbell, 1979) when it is not possible to include all of the elements of experimental design (e.g., randomization), a grounded theory researcher may be able to approximate a grounded theory study. For example, sometimes you cannot use "theoretical sampling" because the accessible population is too small. If there are time limitations, the study might have to end before "theoretical saturation" is reached. If you find yourself in this situation, consider how these limitations might affect your study results, and try to build in mechanisms to address them. In this situation, it is important to state clearly which components of the grounded theory method you were not able to incorporate and why. Also, as you discuss the study's limitations, be sure to consider how these factors may have impacted the findings.

A study on HIV testing provides an excellent example of this type of study (Worthington & Myers, 2003). The authors used data that was collected in an earlier generic qualitative study (Myers et al., 1998), so they were not able to go back to the field to test emerging hypotheses or to conduct theoretical sampling. Sampling for the original study was done using a predetermined stratified sampling strategy with categories such as HIV positive or negative, risk category, region, ethnocultural group, and testing venue. To make up for their inability to do theoretical sampling, the authors created a subsample (39 cases) and used theoretical sampling within that group. To allow for "constant comparison," they first coded within groups of interviews (e.g., HIV negative) until they reached saturation within each group of cases. Ultimately, they identified "anxiety" as their core category, and identified strategies used by the respondents to enhance control in patient-provider relationships. Like many grounded theory studies, their results present a more complex understanding of their topic than was available based on previous research. The authors conclude, "It is also apparent that current social constructionist views of risk are simplistic and do not take into account the more sophisticated (statistical) understandings of risk that are present within the general public" (p. 652).

In introducing the idea of "limited grounded theory" studies, I do not mean to suggest that this term is an appropriate description for any study that uses any of the components of the grounded theory method. As discussed in Chapter 5, my view is that the term "grounded theory" is appropriate only for studies that are designed to build theory. However, it is not always easy to distinguish between what I describe here as "limited grounded theory" study and other types of qualitative research, because qualitative researchers often use components of the grounded theory method to achieve other aims. Nor is it always clear what constitutes a "theory." For example, in a study designed to describe perceptions of the empowerment process, Everett, Homstead, and Drisko (2007) incorporate many of the key components of grounded theory. They develop a series of six stages of the empowerment process, without describing this as a theory of empowerment.Nor is every study that aims to develop theory a grounded theory study, because other qualitative traditions may include theory development, although it is not the primary goal.

My point is not to set up rigid descriptive conventions for grounded theory studies. Instead, I want to encourage researchers to use grounded theory techniques to develop theories, even when they cannot incorporate all components of the grounded theory method. Otherwise, the social work field risks losing the opportunity for theory development to guide social work practice. (See Oktay, Jacobson and Fisher, in press, for an example of a limited grounded theory study.)

ETHICAL ISSUES IN GROUNDED THEORY

Grounded theory researchers today must meet standards for the ethical conduct of qualitative research (Shaw, 2003, 2008). Unfortunately, there is little discussion of ethical issues in the grounded theory literature. In part, this is because the level of awareness and concern about ethical conduct of research is much greater today than it was at the time that grounded theory methods were developed. We have a responsibility to consider potential harm to our respondents, to ensure that we provide informed consent, and to renegotiate consent if it is a lengthy study (Shaw, 2008; Waldrop, 2004). In addition, we must maintain confidentiality and protect privacy (Padgett, 2008). In addition to the responsibilities for ethical conduct of

> Box 6.1 Potential Ethical Concerns in Qualitative Research
>
> - Does it violate principle of informed consent?
> - Does it harm "subjects" through emotional distress?
> - Does it involve damaging information?
> - Does it protect privacy and preserve confidentiality?
> - Does it require a Certificate of Confidentiality?
> - Does it involve vulnerable populations?
> - Does it have the potential for coercion?
>
> Source: Padgett (2008).

concern to all qualitative researchers, social work researchers also have to uphold the values and the ethical code of the profession (see Box 6.1).

The potential for ethical violations varies depending on the nature of the study. It is the researcher's responsibility to assess these carefully and take steps needed to minimize them.

For example, in my breast cancer research, there is potential for emotional distress, because women share their memories of a painful time in their lives. Therefore, I give respondents a list of resources they can use to follow up on any stressful issues that come up in the interviews. I also call them a few days after the interview, to make sure they are not left with residual concerns or strong, unresolved feelings. My interviews could also reveal potentially damaging or embarrassing information, even when names are changed. To prevent this, I routinely give respondents a copy of their "case studies" and any lengthy quotations I plan to use so that they can review them and suggest changes before publication.

Informed consent may be more difficult in grounded theory than in other qualitative designs because it may be hard to explain the goal of theory building in everyday language. Also, informed consent obtained early in the project may no longer be relevant later in the same project because the study focus and the research question are likely to change over the course of the study. For this reason, it is important to include renegotiation of informed consent in the study design.

Grounded Theory and the Institutional Review Board

Some IRBs uses a positivist epistemology and a quantitative research framework, even when reviewing qualitative research. Often, the format for submitting a proposal to the IRB is not appropriate for a grounded theory study. At my institution (which is on a medical campus), research protocols for the IRB must include the following information: rationale for the study, literature review, hypotheses, a detailed description of the sample (how many people, characteristics of the people, inclusion and exclusion criteria), identification of any vulnerable populations, recruitment procedures (including copies of any recruitment materials), data-gathering instruments (a questionnaire is expected), description of the data analysis strategy, and a detailed schedule for the study, showing precisely when data will be gathered and when it will be analyzed. A consent form must be included, with a clear statement of the purpose of the study, how long the interview will last, a list of risks and benefits, and instructions on what to do if harmed. None of this (with the possible exception of the study rationale) is consistent with the grounded theory method. A clear focused research question is not used early in a grounded theory study because it would hem in the researcher and prevent the incorporation of new dimensions that arise in the course of the data gathering. In grounded theory, the literature review should be "sensitizing" and not fixed, and the sampling strategy should follow concepts that only become known through the process of data analysis (theoretical sampling). Because of this type of sampling, the grounded theory researcher cannot always identify vulnerable populations in advance. Also, in grounded theory studies, interview guides should change as the study progresses. Even how long the study will take and how many cases have to be studied depend on theoretical saturation, so this cannot be predicted in advance. Box 6.2 shows problems that an IRB may have with grounded theory research.

The need for IRB approval means that the grounded theory researcher has to reconcile the demands of the IRB and the grounded theory model of research. One strategy I use is to assume that the IRB members are not familiar with grounded theory, and begin with an explanation of the method. Sometimes very hard-nosed quantitative researchers become enthusiastic once they realize that this type of research is designed to generate new theory, and not to test existing theory. Since they recognize that theory is essential for quality quantitative research, they understand the need for new theory in areas where existing theory does not apply. If your epistemological model is consistent with future theory testing using

---

Box 6.2   IRB Problems with Grounded Theory Research

- Broad, open research question (lack of focused question or hypothesis) makes it hard for IRB to weigh risk versus benefit of the study.
- Lack of extensive literature review makes it hard for IRB to evaluate quality of the study.
- Unstructured interview and observation (lack of structured questionnaire) make it difficult for IRB to determine if sensitive or potentially damaging information is involved.
- Theoretical sampling makes it difficult for IRB to determine the characteristics of the respondents and inclusion and exclusion criteria.
- Theoretical saturation makes it hard for you to determine the study schedule and how many respondents you will need to include.

---

traditional (positivist) research methods, this can also be a convincing point (see O'Connor, Netting, & Thomas, 2008).

Another technique is to use language that the IRB members will understand. In my university, since the social work school is on a medical campus, most of the IRB members are physicians or medical researchers, so I describe my study using terms like "pilot study," "natural history," or a "phase one trial."

To deal with the IRB's need for a description of the study population, I specify the characteristics of the population I am going to start with on my IRB application. Since I usually begin sampling using purposeful sampling, I use my "best guess" about what characteristics I am going to need. Later, as my theory develops, if I need to vary from this initial population, I request an amendment, explaining the rationale. In my university, IRBs can take a long time to do an initial review, but they can turn around an amendment very quickly—especially if the changes do not raise any "red flags."

Another technique is to use standards for qualitative research from institutions that are respected by the IRB to help legitimate your study. For example, since I am at a medical campus, the National Institutes of Health (NIH) document on the review of qualitative research applications (NIH, 2001) can be a helpful resource. Hopefully, IRBs will become more familiar with qualitative research and grounded theory in the future, as these models become more accepted.

USING QUALITATIVE SOFTWARE IN GROUNDED THEORY DATA ANALYSIS

Another important consideration for today's researchers that was not available when grounded theory was developed is the use of computer-assisted qualitative data analysis software (CAQDAS) programs in data analysis. A colleague who does quantitative research once asked me the following question, "Did you run your data through NVivo yet?" I had to laugh, because the wording of her question suggested that the computer program would actually do the data analysis for me. It doesn't! Whether you decide to use CAQDAS or not, it is important to remember that these programs do not "think" for you (see Figure 6.1). Ultimately, the quality of your research is going to depend much more on your own ability and effort, and not on whether or not you use CAQDAS. The software does little to prevent bias or "forcing," even if you use the software coder "reliability" programs. Your ability to examine and restrain your own biases is always far more important.

Benefits and Disadvantages of CAQDAS in Grounded Theory Analysis

CAQDAS packages can be useful for some of the data analysis techniques I have discussed in this volume, although they may be less helpful in grounded theory research than in other types of qualitative analysis. In Figure 6.2, I list a number of potential benefits, including coding, memos, data storage and retrieval, searches and queries, diagrams, and audit trail. Another potential benefit, depending on the resources in your setting, is that your data may be accessible to multiple researchers for review or analysis. Also, a CAQDAS project on a secure computer or server that is frequently backed up may be safer than if it were sitting in boxes in your home or office.

Disadvantages of using CAQDAS include the obvious ones (e.g., the costs of purchase, training, and updating as new releases come out and the time costs of learning the program) and costs that are less concrete, which depend on your personality and work style. To get the full benefits of the CAQDAS programs, you may need to spend a lot of time "neatening up" your codes and data as your concepts change. This can be a boring task, and you may find you are spending most of your time doing rote tasks instead of deep and creative thinking. Using CAQDAS takes a lot of the fun out of doing grounded theory research for me, because

"Are we thinking here, or is this just so much pointing and clicking?"

Figure 6.1 *"Are we thinking here?"* Source: © Richard Cline/The New Yorker Collection/www.cartoonbank.com.

I would much rather be working while sitting on the beach or in the woods than in front of my computer. Some researchers may be tempted to use the computer to avoid the hard thinking that is such a central part of grounded theory. Others may end up getting so enthralled with what CAQDAS can do that they let the capability of the program drive the data analysis. Finally, the use of these programs has the potential to distance the researcher from the data. In the end, the decision on whether to use

CAQDAS Functions	Uses in Grounded Theory Analysis
Coding	Make "in vivo codes," substantive or theoretical codes Combine codes into concepts and categories (rename, move codes) Define concepts and categories Create subcodes Create conditions and consequences
Memos	Create memos Attach memos to cases or codes
Data storage and retrieval	Easily locate data and see how it is coded Incorporate documents, audio-files and video-files
Searches and queries	Explore patterns in your data Test preliminary hypotheses Compare coding by different coders
Diagrams	Create a visual model of your theory (relationships between concepts and categories) Move easily between the model and coded data
Audit trail	Keep a record of your data analysis Show how your concepts developed from the data Use your memos to show the development of your ideas
Other	Back up your project and your work Keep your work secure (safeguards) Facilitate multiple researchers viewing and/or contributing to the analysis

Figure 6.2 Potential benefits of using CAQDAS in grounded theory research.

CAQDAS and, if so, how much to use it will be made depending on characteristics of the project itself, the researcher's working style, and the resources of the setting.

Considerations on which CAQDAS Program to Use

In the past, there were substantial differences between these programs (e.g., Atlas.ti was the only one that could handle audio and visual media), but today these programs are all quite similar (see Bazeley, 2007; Lewins & Silver, 2007). Therefore, factors such as the support available at your university (many schools only support one of the qualitative programs), including informal support, such as what other faculty, researchers, and students are using, may be most important. If you are a student, explore any special pricing for students, but be aware of any limitations, such as a limited time period or a limited amount of data that can be saved. Some programs may not be compatible with your computer's operating system, or may require more space than you have available. Finally, if you are doing a large project or a group project, explore the special features of the

CAQDAS, such as its ability to merge projects or to mesh with quantitative statistics software. (See Drisko [2004] for an excellent discussion of CAQDAS for qualitative research in general.)

PUBLISHING GROUNDED THEORY STUDIES

There are many outstanding resources on writing and publishing qualitative research (e.g. Becker, 2007; Drisko, 2005; Padgett, 2008) which are equally relevant to writing up grounded theory research. In this brief section, I focus on some aspects of publishing that can be different for the grounded theory researcher. In grounded theory, the theoretical memos that you have written while doing the analysis form the backbone of your report. Therefore, writing up a grounded theory research project is largely a matter of deciding how you want to "tell the story." The formats for writing up grounded theory research have changed substantially since the original version of grounded theory was developed (Glaser & Strauss, 1967). Consider that the "dying study" resulted in three books. While books and dissertations remain an ideal format for grounded theory studies, social work researchers often want to publish their studies in journals so that their work will be more accessible to practitioners. Today, researchers in academic settings where quantitative research is dominant may find that publications in journals are more valued than are books, since most quantitative researchers rely primarily on journals for their own publications.

However, journals present a number of problems for publishing grounded theory research. First, the page limitations in journals make it difficult to describe the process and the results of a grounded theory study. One strategy is to focus on your most important category or categories, those that you have the most support for, are the most dense, and/or add the most to the field. Another is to divide your findings into several separate journal articles. For example, some authors publish one article on the dimensions of a core category, another article on the relationships among conditions and consequences, and a third article on how to use the theory to enhance social work practice. This strategy can be especially effective if the researcher wants to reach different audiences (e.g., practitioners, researchers). This raises concern that the big picture may be lost as different aspects of the study are broken off into publishable units.

Another problem is that the journal may specify a format for research articles that is based on quantitative research. This is likely to be the case if the journal is not dedicated to publishing only qualitative research. Many social work journals use the American Psychological Association (APA) format, which requires the paper to be organized in a way that doesn't always fit well with grounded theory research. Some compromise is necessary, especially if you are following a version of grounded theory that frowns on any literature review in advance of the research. The format I presented in Chapter 2 for a research proposal can be useful in writing up the results. At the point of publication, however, the original theoretical perspectives and literature review sections need to be revised if they no longer fit with your findings. The task of the grounded theory researcher is to make the article "read" or "flow" in a reasonable way, even though this might not always reflect the order in which the components of the article were done.

The most important factor in any writing project is the audience. When you are writing in a qualitative research journal, you can expect familiarity with grounded theory, and you can focus your attention on your methodology and results. In contrast, many of the audiences in social work will not be knowledgeable about the grounded theory method, so you may need to include some education and explanation in your article. As social work researchers, our most important audience is social work practitioners. We need to invite practitioners in, to help us to test the theory out in real-world settings, adapt it as needed, and put it to work! The task for the grounded theory researcher in social work is to present his or her theory in a way that is understandable and usable to those in practice. This is the true purpose of grounded theory.

In the exemplar studies I used to illustrate the concepts in this book, it was common for authors to publish several articles from the grounded theory studies.

Exemplar #1: Alaggia

The exemplar grounded theory article discussed throughout this volume on maternal support in cases of child sexual abuse (Alaggia, 2002) is actually the second article published from the study. In 2001, Alaggia published a study focusing on one conditional factor in (lack of) maternal support: religion and culture. Alaggia went on to conduct another study on a related topic—the disclosure process of adults who had been sexually abused in childhood (Alaggia, 2004). Then, an article was published, based on combining the findings in the two studies (Alaggia & Turton, 2005). The authors used constant comparison to elucidate another condition of lack of maternal support—this time, a history of domestic violence. In this way, Alaggia continued to develop and expand her theory of maternal support in child sexual abuse.

Exemplar #2: Anderson and Danis

The Anderson and Danis exemplar, too, is part of a body of research that extends beyond the single article used in this volume. In Anderson's case, she developed a broad theory of resistance in different populations. Prior to conducting the 2006 study with Danis, she had completed grounded theory dissertation research on incest survivors. She has since published a book, *Enhancing Resilience in Survivors of Family Violence* (2010), that extends her theoretical framework to battered women as well. Her book is targeted primarily to practitioners, and it emphasizes how to use her theoretical model in practice. More recently, she and Danis have collaborated with Havig to expand the exemplar study, adding additional cases (Anderson, Danis, & Havig, 2011). Anderson and Danis continue to use the grounded theory method to expand their theoretical model and to advance social work practice in their field.

Exemplar #3: Yan

Yan published three journal articles from his dissertation. The first (Yan, 2005) focuses on the concept of culture and crossing, and how social workers from different cultural backgrounds interpret this concept as they interact with clients. Then, he published the exemplar article (2008a), and in the same year, he published another article that provides an overview of the key findings. The different articles focus on different aspects of his study and are targeted at different audiences (Yan, 2008b).

GROUNDED THEORY IN MIXED-METHOD STUDIES

Mixed-method studies incorporate both quantitative and qualitative methodologies.While it is beyond the scope of this book to discuss mixed-method research in depth, I consider how grounded theory can be used in this type of research, since mixed-method research has become attractive to many social work researchers. Like other topics discussed in this chapter, it was not widely used at the time that grounded theory was developed, although Glaser and Strauss (1967), and later, Glaser (1978), incorporated quantitative research into their own grounded theory studies, to "fill in" the logical argument being developed or to verify a grounded theory.

Most mixed-method research does not use grounded theory as the qualitative research model, in part because theory development is not usually the goal of the qualitative component of mixed-method research. Also, grounded theory may be impractical because the timing of a grounded theory study is difficult to predict, making it hard to conduct simultaneously with the quantitative study, and because of the need for theoretical saturation. However, there are some advantages to using grounded theory in mixed-method research. An important one is that it is possible to do grounded theory in a "positivist" or "postpositivist" epistemology. Since this is likely to be the epistemology of the quantitative piece, it can be more compatible than are qualitative methods with a constructivist or postmodern epistemology. In the next section, I provide some examples of different models of mixed-method research in social work that use grounded theory as their qualitative research model.

One mixed-method design that can work with a grounded theory qualitative component is the "sequential" model, especially if the qualitative study is done first and if the qualitative study is seen as dominant (see Creswell & Plano Clark [2007], Greene [2007], and Tashakkori & Teddlie [2003] for discussion of the designs for mixed-method research). In this case, a grounded theory study can be used to develop a theoretical model, and a quantitative study can then be designed based on this theoretical model. An example is the mixed-method study that was designed to develop a quantitative instrument to measure user views of health care that would incorporate the views of dissatisfied patients (Coyle & Williams, 2000). This study began with a grounded theory study of people who had indicated in a previous patient satisfaction survey that they were dissatisfied with hospital services. The grounded theory results were then used to develop a quantitative instrument that would be compatible with the experiences of these users. (See Schmidt et al, in press, for another example of this type of mixed-method research.) A reverse sequential model is also possible, where a grounded theory study is done after a quantitative component is complete. In this case, the grounded theory study can be used to help explain the quantitative results by building a theoretical context.

Concurrent mixed-method studies using grounded theory present several difficulties and are rarely done. An example of a concurrent mixed-method study using grounded theory is the work on perceptions of financial elder abuse and help seeking in an elderly Korean population by Lee and Eaton (2009). In this study, qualitative and quantitative interviews were done back to back. Grounded theory was used to identify views of elder abuse and attitudes toward help seeking, and these were then explored quantitatively to identify demographic characteristics and interactions. I would describe the qualitative component of this study as "limited grounded theory" because there was only one cycle of data gathering and analysis.

Another interesting example of a concurrent mixed-method study design using grounded theory involved the evaluation of a dementia care unit (Morgan & Stewart, 2002). The authors planned a "natural experiment" around a dementia special care unit that was going to be closed, causing the residents to be moved to a unit with fewer residents and more space. They included a qualitative component for purposes of convergence (i.e., to see if an inductive theory would be similar to the one they used in their hypothesis, they developed on the expected impact of the changed physical space). Figures 6.3 and 6.4 show the quantitative conceptual model and the model the authors developed following the qualitative analysis. The model at the end of the grounded theory study suggested a more complex, interactive relationship between the person and the environment than what had been expected using the quantitative model alone. "Results from the study using the qualitative method suggest a need for balance between having too much and too little space. Residents need enough space to move about freely and to maintain control over levels of social interaction, but too much space creates problems (e.g. decreased opportunities for informal social interaction, longer distances to walk, institutional appearance)" (p. 487).

These examples show that while it is possible to use a grounded theory model in a mixed-method context, it is usually what I have referred to as a "limited grounded theory." A full grounded theory study is generally impractical in mixed-method research.

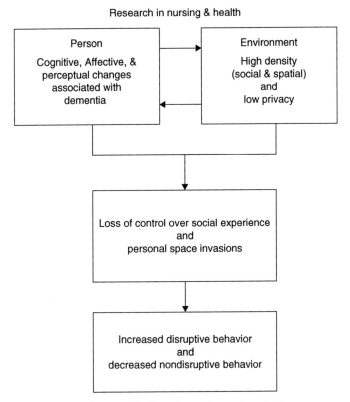

Figure 6.3 Conceptual framework of quasi-experimental method.
Source: Morgan & Stewart (2002).

Combining Grounded Theory and Other Qualitative Traditions

It is also possible to combine grounded theory with other qualitative traditions, as long as the purpose for each methodology is clear. Ethnographic
studies have often included the use of some grounded theory techniques
(Timmermans & Tavory, 2007). Feminist researchers have identified
both plusses and minuses of combining a feminist framework in a
grounded theory study (Olesen, 2007), as have action researchers (Dick,
2007). On the other hand, some qualitative models (e.g., phenomenology, narrative analysis) have very different techniques of data analysis
that may conflict with grounded theory methodology, and they may also

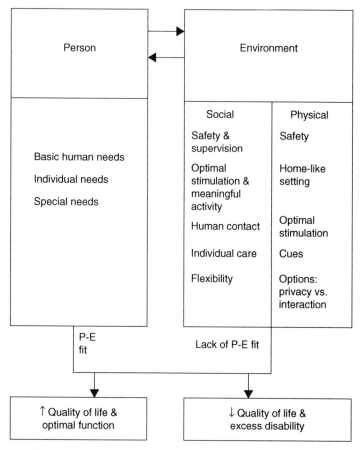

Figure 6.4 Person-environment interaction model. Source: Morgan & Stewart (2002).

have very different goals. These methods are less likely to be successfully combined with grounded theory.

An example of a participatory action research (PAR) study that incorporates a theory development component is provided by Westhues and colleagues (2008). This study is part of a very large Canadian project, "Taking Culture Seriously in Community Mental Health," involving multiple data-gathering methods, four academic disciplines (including social work), and a variety of community participants from different cultural groups. The authors used a community-based format to develop a theoretical framework, and they developed ideas for interventions based directly on this theoretical framework. These interventions were then evaluated using both qualitative and quantitative research methods. Another example of grounded theory combined with other qualitative methods is provided by Ferguson and Islam (2008), who used focus groups in a program evaluation study. While grounded theory logic was used to develop and test hypotheses, the goal was primarily program evaluation by participants (homeless youth), not theory development.

SYNTHESIZING QUALITATIVE RESEARCH: FORMAL GROUNDED THEORY

Formal grounded theory, a grounded theory model for the synthesis of qualitative studies, has been a component of grounded theory from the very beginning (Glaser & Strauss, 1967). Unfortunately, it has been largely ignored and has never been integrated into the grounded theory tradition (Glaser, 2007). Recently, however, qualitative research has come to be accepted as a legitimate component of knowledge building, and it is increasingly sought out in efforts to consolidate current knowledge in a practice area. There is interest in a methodology for qualitative studies that is similar to "meta-analysis," a methodology for synthesizing the findings of quantitative research (Saini & Shlonsky, 2011). The interest in social work and other professions of "evidence-based" and "evidence-informed" practice has increased the demand for quality qualitative studies that can be incorporated into assessments of specific interventions. Formal grounded theory utilizes the same techniques used in grounded theory but synthesizes concepts and categories using studies instead of using raw data. In spite of the fact that it has yet to be utilized in social work research, I discuss formal grounded theory in this chapter, because I think it holds promise for future researchers who aim to synthesize grounded theory studies. (See Paterson, Thorne, Canam, & Jillings [2001] and Saini & Shlonsky [2011] for further information on synthesizing qualitative research.)

Formal grounded theory was described by Glaser and Strauss in *Discovery* (1967) as a way to move beyond "substantive" theory, or theory in a particular area, setting, or field of practice, to a higher level of abstraction. In their research, they considered "dying" to be an example of a broader social process they called an "unscheduled status passage." Moving from a focus on "dying" to a focus on "status passage" is to shift from "substantive" to "formal" theory. The formal theory is not only more abstract but also applicable to a broader range of contexts as it describes a "basic social process." Glaser and Strauss (1967) illustrate how the techniques of grounded theory analysis (identification of concepts, generation of dimensions and properties of concepts, theoretical sampling, and, especially, constant comparison) are used to generate formal grounded theory, either in a single substantive area or across multiple areas, using their concept of "awareness contexts" from the dying study.

The work of Margaret Kearney, a nurse who studied with Glaser and Strauss, provides an illustration of formal grounded theory. Kearney has synthesized qualitative studies in two substantive areas, battered women and women's recovery from drug abuse, using the formal grounded theory method (Kearney 2007). In her synthesis of qualitative studies on battered women (2001), she states that the goal of a "formal grounded theory" is "substantive grounded-theory studies are synthesized to develop a higher-level grounded theory" (p. 271). To develop a formal grounded theory, she first identified a set of grounded theory studies in the substantive area, based on clear criteria for inclusion and exclusion. She then applied the constant comparative method to the studies. Grounded theory methods were used to generate a core theory. In her synthesis in the field of domestic violence, Kearney identified 13 studies, most of them using grounded theory methodology, with a total of 282 women who were participants in these studies. Using grounded theory methods, she identified a core category of "enduring love," which she describes as "a continual struggle to redefine partner violence as temporary, survivable, or reasonable by adhering to values of commitment and self-sacrifice in the relationship and by using strategies to survive and control the psychic and physical harm of the unpredictable" (p. 275). Kearney also identified four stages of the process these women go through as they shift the focus of their love from their abusive partners to their children and themselves: "This is what I wanted," "The more I do the worse I am," "I had enough," and "I was finding me." Note that Kearney uses the words of the respondents to title these phases.

Formal grounded theory is dependent upon the existence of a set of studies in a similar problem area, field, or population. This may be hard to find, since most qualitative studies are not theory-generating studies.

Studies that have not developed concepts and categories cannot be combined or synthesized using grounded theory techniques. Even if they are solid grounded theory studies, it may not be possible to create a synthesis if they focus on different time periods or phases of an experience or are done in very different circumstances or settings. This is illustrated by the work of Thorne and Paterson (1998), who tried to synthesize qualitative studies on chronic illness over several decades. A synthesis was not possible because the earlier studies focused on the stress and the burdens created by the illness, while the later studies focused on the rewards. Until we build up a body of solid grounded theory research in specific substantive areas, formal grounded theory is not feasible. Since synthesis of qualitative findings is based on an assumption that a synthesis of common findings across many studies comes closer to reality or truth than the results of any single study, it is more likely to be valued by those grounded theory researchers who are comfortable with positivist, postpositivist, or pragmatic assumptions than those with constructionist or postmodern worldviews. In spite of these problems, I believe that it has great promise for the synthesis of grounded theory studies in social work in the future.

THE PROMISE OF GROUNDED THEORY RESEARCH IN SOCIAL WORK

In this chapter, I have discussed grounded theory research today in light of a number of recent developments in social work research. Many of these reflect changes in the research environment since grounded theory was developed almost 50 years ago. I have discussed some of the difficulties doing grounded theory studies today, and how a limited grounded theory model can sometimes be used if it is clearly described and the researcher takes the limitations into consideration in his or her study design. I also discussed issues of ethics in qualitative research, IRB requirements, the use of computer software, publication of grounded theory studies, mixed-method designs, and formal grounded theory. While none of these subjects was discussed in depth, I felt it important to familiarize those interested in grounded theory of their potential.

Grounded theory has survived for almost 50 years, in part because of its flexibility, and because its goal (theory development) remains important. I have argued throughout this pocket guide that the development of practice-relevant theory is as important to social work today as it ever was. Although grounded theory has been available to social work researchers for many years and is one of the more popular of the qualitative research methods, I feel that it has not yet fulfilled its full potential in social work. It is my hope that in this volume, I have helped the reader to understand the grounded theory method, where it came from, how it is done, how it should be evaluated, and how it can be used in today's research context. I hope, too, that I have been able to communicate my enthusiasm for this methodology and my conviction that it has much to offer to the social work profession. The goal of grounded theory is to produce theories that can be used in practice, with the ideal being a practitioner and a researcher working together to develop, shape, and put theory into practice. Social work researchers may need to look back to our roots to "rediscover" that grounded theory methodology fits so well with the person-in-environment worldview. This methodology has the potential to develop social work theories that are relevant to practice. In this way can we have practice that is rooted in theory. It is this vision that makes me so excited about the contribution that grounded theory can make to social work.

CHAPTER SUMMARY

This chapter discussed how grounded theory is affected by a variety of recent developments in social work research, including why it is sometimes difficult to conduct a grounded theory study today, and what to do when you want to develop theory, but it is impractical to apply the grounded theory method as it has been described in the previous chapters of this volume. The chapter also considered ethical and IRB issues in grounded theory research. I discussed some of the practical considerations in publishing grounded theory studies, with illustrations from exemplar grounded theory studies. The use of computer software programs in grounded theory analysis and use of grounded theory in mixed method research were also discussed. Chapter 6 also includes a brief description of 'formal grounded theory', the grounded theory model for synthesizing qualitative studies. Finally, I argue that grounded theory has much to offer social work today, and encourage readers to further explore (and hopefully contribute to) the rich field of grounded theory research in social work. Exercises designed to help readers apply the material in the chapter to their own research are provided.

SUGGESTED EXERCISES

1. Examine the format for a dissertation proposal at your institution (if you are a PhD student) or a grant proposal from an agency you aspire to get funded by (if you are a faculty member or researcher). What is expected in the proposal? For each area, consider whether this is possible, or desirable, if you are doing a grounded theory study. What strategies might you want to adopt to handle any discrepancies? (You might want to look at some proposals from others [students or researchers] who have done grounded theory studies at your institution, or from other researchers who have gotten grounded theory studies funded by the funding agency.)

2. Examine the methodology of your own grounded theory study or published studies in your area of interest that use the term "grounded theory" to describe their methodology. Discuss whether these actually are grounded theory studies, or perhaps "limited grounded theory" studies, or a more generic form of qualitative analysis. If you consider it a "limited grounded theory" study, consider what might be the weaknesses of the study. What could you do to strengthen the study and limit these weaknesses?

3. (If you are at an institution that has an IRB) Examine the format that is required for a protocol from your IRB. Consider how this does or does not fit with a grounded theory proposal. What strategies might you want to adopt to handle any discrepancies? (Find out how receptive your IRB is to qualitative research, and whether it has approved grounded theory studies in the past.)

4. Download trial versions (free) of the CAQDAS programs. Repeat exercise #1, but this time, use the programs to create your codes, concepts, and memos. Consider what you found to be the advantages and disadvantages of each method.

5. Examine the three studies I have used in this pocket guide as exemplar grounded theory social work studies. Consider how the

authors "told the story" of their study. Did they have to adjust to a format that does not reflect grounded theory methods? Did the writing "flow"? Was it understandable and applicable for practice? If not, how could it have been written so that it would be more compelling to practitioners?

6. Find some mixed-method studies in your field of interest. Identify the type of mixed-method model that was used. Do any of these use grounded theory for the qualitative method? Would it have been a good idea if they had? Or would this have been impractical, or a poor fit with the study purpose?

Glossary

Abduction a type of reasoning used in grounded theory research that combines inductive and deductive logic in a cyclic process of theory development. As theory is derived inductively from the data, it is confirmed deductively by seeking and examining additional data.

Applicability in grounded theory, a theory is evaluated by whether or not it is applicable to practice. To meet the criteria of applicability, a theory must fit the practice setting, be understandable to those in the practice setting, be applicable to a broad variety of settings, and advance the practitioner's control of the practice situation.

Audit trail a compendium of documents, such as researcher journals, memos, etc., that illustrate and support the researcher's decision-making process from research conceptualization to final data analysis.

Axial coding a set of coding techniques used in grounded theory to move the analysis from description to theory building. Axial coding involves identifying conditions, actions/interactions, and consequences; relating a category to its subcategories; and looking for cues in the data about how major categories relate to each other. In grounded theory, this process allows the researcher to bring the data together after open coding has broken it apart.

CAQDAS an acronym for "computer-assisted qualitative data analysis software." Two widely used programs are NVivo and Atlas.ti. Caution should always be used when using computer analytics, as software analysis is not an adequate substitute for human analysis.

Categories concepts that go together and are identified as important in the analysis are combined into categories. Categories are important in all levels of coding in grounded theory analysis. They are identified in open coding, and they are further explored in axial coding and related to other categories. Selective coding involves the identification of a core category that is central to the theory.

Coding the process of analyzing data by identifying common elements or patterns. In grounded theory, coding results from the constant comparison of data and analytic concepts and categories. This comparative process allows for the disaggregation of large amounts of data into smaller, more manageable groups of ideas or concepts. Coding goes on throughout the grounded theory analysis and should be considered to be fluid, dynamic, and organic. Coding is initially tied closely to the data, but becomes increasingly abstract as the analysis progresses.

Concepts groups of codes that go together to embody an idea. Concepts are the building blocks of theory.

Conceptual framework as specified by Maxwell (2005), a conceptual framework includes a problem statement, experience with the topic, relevant theory(ies), review of prior research, and thought experiments. A concept map is a useful device to specify an initial conceptual framework. This notion is similar to the idea of theoretical sensitivity in grounded theory.

Constant comparative method a technique used to develop grounded theory that involves comparing sets of data to other data (case to case, incident to incident), as well as comparing data to concepts and categories, and comparing concepts and categories to each other. Constant comparison is used to identify both similarities and differences. It contributes to the generation and development of conceptual categories. Through the application of constant comparison, along with additional data collection, the theory becomes increasingly abstract.

Constructivism an epistemological approach based on the view that all reality is constructed. In this view, participants construct their views and realities. The researcher, too, recognizes that the grounded theory produced in the study is also a construction.

Core category in selective coding, a core category is identified based on its frequency in the data, its abstract nature, and its explanatory power in relation to other categories. (See "selective coding.")

Credibility a criterion for evaluating the quality of a grounded theory study. A theory will be credible to the extent that the grounded theory method was appropriately and carefully applied.

Deduction a type of reasoning that begins with preexisting theory and uses data to verify or test the theory.

Dimension variations of a property of a concept or category.

Formal grounded theory a more abstract level of theory development allowing for the application of a substantive theory to broader phenomena or contexts. Formal grounded theory uses grounded theory techniques to synthesize a set of comparable grounded theory studies.

Grounded theory a form of inquiry, based on symbolic interactionism, that develops middle-range theory through a multistage process of data-gathering and data analysis. Techniques used in grounded theory include constant comparison, theoretical sampling, (application of) theoretical sensitivity, and theoretical saturation.

Induction a type of reasoning that begins with data and develops descriptive or analytic concepts from the data.

Limited grounded theory a study that aims to develop theory and uses grounded theory techniques but in which issues, such as limited sample or use of secondary qualitative data, preclude the full use of grounded theory methodology. A researcher who conducts a limited grounded theory study needs to consider the potential impact of the lack of the limitations on the study results and seek ways to compensate for these.

Member checking a technique used to enhance trustworthiness in qualitative research in which the researcher consults with participants concerning the accuracy of the data and the findings.

Memos/memoing a researcher's record of thoughts, ideas, and questions concerning the developing theory. In grounded theory, it is important to begin memoing as soon as the study begins. Memos become increasingly abstract as categories are identified and elaborated in the analysis. They ultimately form the basis of the final reports and papers. Memos are an important component of the "audit trail" (above) used to establish trustworthiness.

Negative case analysis the intentional search for cases or incidents that could disconfirm the developing theory. Negative case analysis is used late in grounded theory analysis to challenge tentative hypotheses. If a negative case is found, this may serve to further theory development by adding conditions or contexts where the hypothesis does not apply. On the other hand, failure to find a negative case may substantiate the legitimacy of the researcher's hypotheses.

Open coding the first stage of grounded theory analysis, open coding involves breaking down or splitting up the data into segments through line-by-line examination of data and labeling the segments using a word or words that convey meaning. Open coding identifies concepts and their dimensions and properties, and includes consolidation of concepts with other concepts into larger categories.

Peer debriefing a technique used in qualitative research to enhance trustworthiness, peer debriefing refers to the process of reviewing elements of the research with others who can provide critical feedback to the researcher.

Positivism an epistemology indicative of the acceptance of a "knowable reality" (naïve realism) in which the researcher is viewed as an objective observer. Research in this model aims to discover universal laws that can be used for purposes of explanation and prediction.

Pragmatism an American philosophy espousing that something is true if it is useful and practically applicable.

Prolonged engagement a technique used to enhance trustworthiness in qualitative research, prolonged engagement involves engagement with the data for a long enough time to reduce respondent bias and reactivity to the presence of the researcher.

Property a characteristic of a concept or category.

Reflexivity a technique to enhance trustworthiness in qualitative research in which the researcher explores his or her own experiences, opinions, and assumptions and considers how these may impact the findings. A reflexive journal can be used to add reflexivity to a grounded theory study.

Relationality a technique used in participatory action research in which the community is intentionally involved in the research process. The incorporation of an active community advisory board can add relationality to a grounded theory study.

Selective coding an advanced stage in grounded theory analysis where a core category is identified as central to the theory. Selective coding also involves development of the core category to the point of saturation. In addition, selective coding includes specification of the relationship between the core category and other categories that constitute the theory.

Substantive codes (in vivo) codes based directly on the data, and not on previously identified theory. (See "theoretical coding.") "In vivo" codes are a type of substantive code that use the exact words or ideas of the respondent in the code title or label.

Symbolic interactionism a theoretical perspective based on the work of G. Herbert Mead that focuses on the interaction between the individual and the environment, resulting in shared symbols and meanings. Individuals are seen as actively involved in shaping their environments.

Theoretical codes codes that are based on abstract concepts. Researchers need to be wary of using theoretical codes until they are reasonably certain that they are grounded in the data, and not imposed by the researcher. Theoretical codes can help the researcher link the theory to existing theory.

Theoretical sampling theoretical sampling involves the selection of study participants, incidents, and settings based on the need to develop emerging theory by exploring the dimensions and properties of the theoretical categories.

Theoretical saturation theoretical saturation occurs when comparison of new data elicits no new theoretical information (i.e., no new properties, dimensions, conditions, actions/interactions, or consequences are seen).

Theoretical sensitivity a characteristic of the researcher that enables theory to be recognized or developed from data. Theoretical sensitivity is based on the prior experience and knowledge of the researcher.

Triangulation a technique used to enhance trustworthiness in qualitative research, triangulation involves the inclusion of more than one type of data, theory, method, or observer.

Trustworthiness a term used in qualitative research to parallel the term "validity" in quantitative research. Techniques such as prolonged engagement, member checking, peer debriefing, triangulation, and audit trails are used to enhance the trustworthiness and credibility of qualitative research.

References

Addams, J., ed. (1895, reprinted in 2006). *Hull-House maps and papers: A presentation of nationalities and wages in a congested district of Chicago, together with comments and essays on problems growing out of the social conditions.* Urbana and Chicago: University of Illinois Press.

Alaggia, R. (2001). Cultural and religious influences in maternal response to intrafamilial child sexual abuse: Charting new territory for research and treatment. *Journal of Child Sexual Abuse, 10*(2), 41–60.

Alaggia, R. (2002). Balancing acts: Reconceptualizing support in maternal response to intra-familial child sexual abuse. *Clinical Social Work Journal, 30*(1), 41–56.

Alaggia, R. (2004). Many ways of telling: Expanding conceptualization of child sexual abuse disclosure. *Child Abuse and Neglect, 28*(11), 1213–1227.

Alaggia, R., & Turton, J. (2005). Against the odds: The impact of woman abuse on maternal response to disclosure of child sexual abuse. *Journal of Child Sexual Abuse, 14*(4), 95–113.

Anderson, K. M. (2010). *Enhancing resilience in survivors of family violence.* New York, NY: Springer Publishing Company.

Anderson, K., & Danis, F. (2006). Adult daughters of battered women: Resistance and resilience in the face of danger. *Affilia, 21*(4), 419–432.

Anderson, K. M., Danis, F. S., & Havig, K. (2011). Adult daughters of battered women: Recovery and posttraumatic growth following childhood adversity. *Families in Society, 92*(2), 154–160.

Annells, M. (1996). Grounded theory method: Philosophical perspectives, paradigm of inquiry and postmodernism. *Qualitative Health Research, 6*(3), 379–393.

Bazeley, P. (2007). *Qualitative data analysis with NVIVO.* Los Angeles, CA: Sage Publications, Inc.

Becker, H. (1998). *Tricks of the trade: How to think about your research while doing it.* Chicago, IL: University of Chicago Press.

Becker, H. (2007) *Writing for social scientists: How to start and finish your thesis, book or article.* Chicago, IL: University of Chicago Press.

Birks, M. & Mills, J. (2011) *Grounded theory: A practical guide.* Thousand Oaks, CA: Sage Publications, Inc.

Blumer, H. (1969). *Symbolic interactionism: Perspective and method.* Englewood Cliffs, NJ: Prentice Hall.

Bulmer, M. (1984). *The Chicago School of Sociology: Institutionalization, diversity and the rise of sociological research.* Chicago, IL: University of Chicago Press.

Burstein, J., & Anderson, K. (2011). *Spark: How creativity works.* New York: HarperCollins.

Charmaz, K. (1993). *Good days, bad days: The self in chronic illness and time.* Chapel Hill, NC: Rutgers University Press.

Charmaz, K. (2006). *Constructing grounded theory: A practical guide through qualitative analysis.* Thousand Oaks, CA: Sage Publications, Inc.

Charmaz, K. (2011). Grounded theory methods in social justice research. In N. Denzin & Y. Lincoln (Eds.) *The Sage handbook of qualitative research* (pp. 359–380). Thousand Oaks, CA: Sage Publications, Inc.

Clarke, A. E. (2005). *Situational analysis.* Thousand Oaks, CA: Sage Publications, Inc.

Clarke, A., & Friese, C. (2007). Grounded theorizing using situational analysis. In A. Bryant & K. Charmaz (Eds.), *The Sage handbook of grounded theory* (pp. 363–397). Thousand Oaks, CA: Sage Publications, Inc.

Cook, D. T., & Campbell, T. D. (1979). *Quasi-experimentation designs and analysis issues for field settings.* New York, NY: Houghton Mifflin Press.

Cook, G. A. (1993). *George Herbert Mead: The making of a social pragmatist.* Urbana, IL: University of Illinois Press.

Corbin, J., & Strauss, A. (1988). *Unending work and care: Managing chronic illness in the home.* San Francisco, CA: Jossey-Bass.

Corbin, J., & Strauss, A. (2008). *Basics of qualitative research* (3rd ed.). Thousand Oaks, CA: Sage Publications, Inc.

Coyle, J., & Williams, B. (2000). An exploration of the epistemological intricacies of using qualitative data to develop a quantitative measure of user views of health care. *Journal of Advanced Nursing, 31*(5), 1235–1243.

Crabtree, B., & Miller, W. (1992). A template approach to test analysis: Developing and using codebooks. In B. Crabtree & W. Miller (Eds.), *Doing qualitative research* (pp. 93-109). Newbury Park, CA: Sage Publications, Inc.

Creswell, J. (2007). *Qualitative inquiry and research design: Choosing among five approaches* (2nd ed.). Thousand Oaks, CA: Sage Publications, Inc.

Creswell, J., & Plano Clark, V. L. (2007). *Designing and conducting mixed methods research*. Thousand Oaks, CA: Sage Publications, Inc.

Deegan, J. (2005). *Jane Addams and the men of the Chicago school (1892 – 1918)*. New Brunswick, NJ: Transaction Press.

Dey, I. (1993). *Qualitative data analysis: A user-friendly guide*. London: Routledge.

Dick, B. (2007). What can grounded theorists and action researchers learn from each other? In A. Bryant & K. Charmaz (Eds.), *The Sage handbook of grounded theory* (pp. 398–416). Thousand Oaks, CA: Sage Publications, Inc.

Drisko, J. W. (1997). Strengthening qualitative studies and reports: Standards to enhance academic integrity. *Journal of Social Work Education, 33*, 187–197.

Drisko, J. W. (2004). Qualitative data analysis software: A user's appraisal. In D. Padgett (Ed.), *The qualitative research experience* (rev. ed., pp. 193–209). Belmont, CA: Wadsworth.

Drisko, J. W. (2005). Writing up qualitative research. *Families in Society: The Journal of Contemporary Social Services, 86*(4), 589–593.

Epstein, I. (2010). *Clinical data-mining: Integrating practice and research*. New York, NY: Oxford University Press.

Everett, J. E., Homstead, K., & Drisko, J. (2007). Frontline worker perceptions of the empowerment process in community-based agencies. *Social Work, 52*(2), 161–170.

Ferguson, K. M., & Islam, N. (2008). Conceptualizing outcomes with street-living young adults: Grounded theory approach to evaluating the Social Enterprise Intervention. *Qualitative Social Work, 7*, 217–237.

Forte, J. A. (2004). Symbolic interactionism and social work: A forgotten legacy. *Families in Society, 85*(3), 391–400.

Geertz, C. (1973). Thick description: Towards an interpretive theory of culture. In G. Geertz (Ed.), *The interpretation of cultures* (pp. 3–32). New York, NY: Basic Books.

Gilgun, J. (1994). Hand into glove: The grounded theory approach and social work practice research. In E. Sherman & W. Reid (Eds.), *Qualitative research in social work* (pp. 115–125). New York, NY: Columbia University Press.

Gilgun, J. (1999). Methodological pluralism and qualitative family research. *In* S. K. Steinmetz, M. B. Sussman, & G. W. Peterson (Eds.), *Handbook of marriage and the family* (2nd ed., pp 219–261). New York, NY: Plenum.

Gilgun, J. (2007). *The legacy of the Chicago School of Sociology for family theory building*. Paper presented at the annual conference of the National Council on Family Relations, Nov 7, 2007. Pittsburgh, PA.

Glaser, B., & Strauss A. (1965). *Awareness of dying.* Chicago, IL: Aldine Publishing Company.

Glaser, B., & Strauss, A. (1968). *Time for dying.* Chicago, IL: Aldine Publishing Company.

Glaser, B. (1978). *Theoretical sensitivity.* Mill Valley, CA: Sociology Press.

Glaser, B. (1992). *Basics of grounded theory analysis: Emergence vs. forcing.* Mill Valley, CA: Sociology Press.

Glaser, B. *(2007).* Doing formal theory. In A. Bryant & K. Charmaz (Eds.), *The Sage handbook of grounded theory* (pp. 97–113). Los Angeles, CA: Sage.

Glaser, B., & Strauss, A. (1967). *The discovery of grounded theory.* Chicago, IL: Aldine Publishing Company.

Goffman, E. (1963). *Stigma: Notes on the management of spoiled identity.* New York, NY: Prentice-Hall Publishing.

Greene, J. C. (2007). *Mixed methods in social inquiry.* San Francisco, CA: John Wiley & Sons.

Greene, R. & Ephross, P. (1991). *Human behaviour theory and social work practice.* Mouton De Gruyter.

Hall, W., & Callery, P. (2001). Enhancing the rigor of grounded theory: Incorporating reflexivity and relationality. *Qualitative Health Research, 11*(2), 257–272.

Hartman, A. (1990). Many ways of knowing. *Social Work, 35*(1), 3.

Hood, J. C. (2007). Orthodoxy vs. power: The defining traits of grounded theory. *In* A. Bryant & K. Charmaz (Eds.), *The Sage handbook of grounded theory* (pp. 151–164*).* Thousand Oaks, CA: Sage Publications, Inc.

Kearney, M. (2001). Enduring love: A grounded formal theory of women's experience of domestic violence. *Research in Nursing and Health, 24*(4), 270–282.

Kearney, M. *(2007).* From the sublime to the meticulous: The continuing evolution of grounded formal theory. In A. Bryant & K. Charmaz (Eds.), *The Sage handbook of grounded theory* (pp. 114–126). Thousand Oaks, CA: Sage Publications, Inc.

Kelle, U. *(2007).* The development of categories: Different approaches to grounded theory. In A. Bryant & K. Charmaz (Eds.), *The Sage handbook of grounded theory* (pp. 191–214). Thousand Oaks, CA: Sage Publications, Inc.

Knight, L. *(2010).* *Jane Addams: Spirit in action.* New York, NY: W.W. Norton & Company, Inc.

Lee, H., & Eaton, C. (2009). Financial abuse in elderly Korean immigrants: Mixed analysis of the role of culture on perception and help-seeking intention. *Journal of Gerontological Social Work, 52*(5), 463–488.

Lewins, A., & Silver, C. (2007). *Using software in qualitative research: A step-by-step guide.* Thousand Oaks, CA: Sage Publications, Inc.

Lincoln, Y., & Guba, E. (1985). *Naturalistic inquiry*. Beverly Hills, CA: Sage Publications, Inc.

Locke, K. *(2007)*. Rational control and irrational free-play: Dual-thinking modes as necessary tension in grounded theorizing. In A. Bryant & K. Charmaz (Eds.), *The Sage handbook of grounded theory* (pp. 565–580). Thousand Oaks, CA: Sage Publications, Inc.

Lofland, J., Snow, D., Anderson, L., & Lofland, L. *(2006)*. *Analyzing social settings: A guide to qualitative observation and analysis*. Belmont, CA: Wadsworth & Thomson.

Matarese, M. (2010). An exploration of sexual minority youth experiences in out-of-home care. Unpublished manuscript.

Maxwell, J. (2005). *Qualitative research design: An interactive approach*. Thousand Oaks, CA: Sage Publications, Inc.

McDermid, D. (2006). *Pragmatism*. Retrieved January 29, 2009, from http://www.iep.utm.edu/p/pragmati.htm.

Melia, K. M. (1996). Rediscovering Glaser. *Qualitative Health Research, 6*(3), 368–378.

Merton, R. C. (1968). *Social theory and social structure, 2nd edition*. Glencoe, IL: The Free Press.

Miles, M., & Huberman, A. (1994). *Qualitative data analysis: An expanded sourcebook* (2nd ed.). Thousand Oaks, CA: Sage Publications, Inc.

Morgan, D. G., & Stewart, N. J. (2002). Theory building through mixed-method evaluation of a dementia special care unit. *Research in Nursing and Health, 25*, 479–488.

Morris, C. (Ed.). (1967). *Mind, self and society: From the standpoint of a social behaviorist (Works of George Herbert Mead, Vol. 1)*. Chicago, IL: University of Chicago Press.

Morrow, S. (2005). Quality and trustworthiness in qualitative research in counseling psychology. *Journal of Counseling Psychology, 52*, 250–260.

Morrow, S., & Smith, M. (1995). Constructions of survival and coping by women who have survived childhood sexual abuse. *Journal of Counseling Psychology, 42*, 24–33.

Morse, J., Stern, P., Corbin, J., Bowers, B., Charmaz, K., & Clark, A. (2009). *Developing grounded theory: The second generation*. Walnut Creek, CA: Left Coast Press.

Mruck, K., & Mey, G. *(2007)*. Grounded theory and reflexivity. *In* A. Bryant & K. Charmaz (Eds.), *The Sage handbook of grounded theory (pp. 515–528)*. Thousand Oaks, CA: Sage Publications, Inc.

Myers, T., Haubrich, D., Mahoney, D., Calzavara, L., Cockerill, R., Millson, P., et al. *(1998)*. *The HIV test experience study*. Toronto: HIV Social Behavioural and Epidemiological Studies Unit, Faculty of Medicine, University of Toronto.

National Institutes of Health. (2001). *Qualitative methods in health research: Opportunities and considerations in application and review.* NIH Publication No. 02-!5046, December 2001.

O'Connor, M., Netting, F., & Thomas, M. (2008). Grounded theory: Managing the challenge for those facing institutional review board oversight. *Qualitative Inquiry, 14*(1), 28–45.

Oktay, J. S. & Walter, C. A. (1991) *Breast cancer in the life course : Women's experiences* New York: NY, Springer.

Oktay, J. S. *(2004).* Grounded theory. Part I: Experiences of women whose mothers had breast cancer. Part II: The personal and professional experiences of doing a grounded theory project. In: D. K. Padgett (Ed.), *The qualitative research experience* (pp. 23–47). New York, NY: Wadsworth.

Oktay, J. S. (2005). *Breast cancer: Daughters tell their stories.* New York, NY: Haworth.

Oktay, J. S. (2006) *Standards for quality in grounded theory research.* Annual meeting of the Society for Social Work and Research. San Antonio, TX.

Oktay, J. S., Jacobson, J., & Fisher, L. (in press). Learning by experience: Teaching experiences of social work doctoral students. *Journal of Social Work Education.*

Olesen, V. L. *(2007).* Feminist qualitative research and grounded theory: Complexities, criticisms, and opportunities. In A. Bryant & K. Charmaz (Eds.), *The Sage handbook of grounded theory* (pp. 417–435). Thousand Oaks, CA: Sage Publications, Inc.

Padgett, D. (1998a). Does the glove really fit? Qualitative research and clinical social work practice. *Social Work, 43*(4), 373–381.

Padgett, D. (2004) (Ed.). *The qualitative research experience.* New York, NY: Wadsworth.

Padgett, D. (1998b). *Qualitative methods in social work research: Challenges and rewards.* Thousand Oaks, CA: Sage Publications, Inc.

Padgett, D. (2008). *Qualitative methods in social work research* (2nd ed.). Thousand Oaks, CA: Sage Publications, Inc.

Park-Lee, E. (2005). Creating harmony, creating happiness: Subjective well-being of older Koreans in the U.S. Unpublished dissertation.

Paterson, B. L., Thorne, S. E., Canam C., & Jillings, C. (2001). *Meta-study of qualitative health research: A practical guide to meta-analysis and meta-synthesis.* Thousand Oaks, CA: Sage Publications, Inc.

Quenk, N. R. (2009). *Essentials of Myers-Briggs type indicator assessment (essentials of psychological assessment).* New York, NY: Wiley.

Reichertz, J. *(2007).* Abduction in grounded theory. In A. Bryant & K. Charmaz (Eds.), *The Sage handbook of grounded theory* (pp. 214–228). Thousand Oaks, CA: Sage Publications, Inc.

Richardson, R., & Kramer, E. (2006). Abduction as the type of inference that characterizes the development of a grounded theory. *Qualitative Research, 6*(4), 497–513.

Ritzer, G. (2010a). *Classical sociological theory* (6th ed.). New York, NY: McGraw Hill.

Ritzer, G. (2010b). *Sociological theory* (8th ed.). New York: McGraw Hill.

Robbins, S., Chatterjee, P., & Canda, E. (2006). *Contemporary human behavior theory: A critical perspective for social work* (2nd ed.). Boston, MA: Allyn and Bacon.

Rodwell, M. K. (1998). *Social work constructivist research.* New York, NY: Garland Publishing, Inc.

Saini, M., & Shlonsky, A. (2011). *Systematic synthesis of qualitative research.* New York, NY: Oxford University Press.

Sandelowski, M., & Barroso, J. (2003). Classifying the findings in qualitative studies. *Qualitative Health Research, 13*(7), 905–923.

Schmidt, J. L., Castellanos-Brown, K., Dulshieva, S., Oktay, J. S.,Bonhomme, N., Davidoff, A., Terry, S. & Greene, C. (in press). *Genetics in Medicine.*

Shaw, I. (2003). Ethics in qualitative research and evaluation. *Journal of Social Work, 3*(1), 9–19.

Shaw, I. (2008). Ethics and the practice of qualitative research. *Qualitative Social Work, 7*(4), 400–414.

Star, S. (2007). Living grounded theory: Cognitive and emotional forms of pragmatism. In A. Bryant & K. Charmaz (Eds.), *The Sage handbook of grounded theory* (pp. 75–93). Thousand Oaks, CA: Sage Publications, Inc.

Stern, P. N. (2009). In the beginning Glaser and Strauss. In J. M. Morse, P. N. Stern, J. Corbin, B. Bowers, K. Charmaz, & A. E. Clarke (Eds.), *Developing grounded theory: The second generation* (pp. 24–29). Walnut Creek, CA: Left Coast Press.

Stern, P. N., & Porr, C. J. (2011). *Essentials of accessible grounded theory.* Walnut Creek, CA: Left Coast Press.

Strauss, A. & Mead, G. (1956). *The social psychology of George Herbert Mead.* Chicago: University of Chicago Press.

Strauss, A. (1987). *Qualitative analysis for social scientists.* Cambridge, MA: Cambridge University Press.

Strauss, A. (Ed.). (1977). *George Herbert Mead: On social psychology.* Chicago, IL: University of Chicago Press.

Strauss, A., & Corbin, J. (1990). *Basics of qualitative research.* Newbury Park, CA: Sage Publications, Inc.

Strauss, A., & Corbin, J. (1998). *Basics of qualitative research.* 2nd edition Newbury Park, CA: Sage Publications, Inc.

Strauss, A., Corbin, J., Fagerhaugh, S., Glaser, B., Maines, D., Suczed, B., & Wiener, C. (1984) *Chronic illness and the quality of life.* St. Louis, MO: C.V.Mosby Co.

Strubing, J. (2007). Research as pragmatic problem-solving: The pragmatist roots of empirically-grounded theorizing. In A. Bryant & K. Charmaz (Eds.), *The Sage handbook of grounded theory* (pp. 580–602). Thousand Oaks, CA: Sage Publications, Inc.

Tashakkori, A., & Teddlie, C. (1998). *Mixed methodology: Combining qualitative and quantitative approaches.* Thousand Oaks, CA: Sage Publications, Inc.

Tashakkori, A., & Teddlie, C. (Eds.). (2003). *Handbook of mixed methods in social and behavioral research.* Thousand Oaks, CA: Sage Publications, Inc.

Thorne, S. E., & Paterson, B. (1998). Shifting images of chronic illness. *Image: Journal of Nursing Scholarship, 30,* 173–178.

Thyer, B. A. (1994). Are theories for practice necessary? No! *Journal of Social Work Education, 30,* 148–151.

Thyer, B. A. (2001). The role of theory in research on social work practice. *Journal of Social Work Education, 37,* 9–25.

Timmermans, S., & Tavory, I. (2007) Advancing ethnographic research through grounded theory practice. In A. Bryant & K. Charmaz (Eds.), *The Sage handbook of grounded theory* (pp. 493–512). Thousand Oaks, CA: Sage Publications, Inc.

Waldrop, D. (2004). Ethical issues in qualitative research with high-risk populations: Handle with care. In D. K. Padgett (Ed.), *The qualitative research experience.* (pp 236–249). Belmont, CA: Wadsworth.

Wells, K. (1995). The strategy of grounded theory: Possibilities and problems. *Social Work Research, 19*(1), 33–40.

Wells, K. (2011). *Narrative inquiry.* New York, NY: Oxford University Press.

Westhues, A., Ochocka, J., Jacobson, N., Simich, L., Maiter, S., Janzen, R., & Fleras, A. (2008). Developing theory from complexity: Reflections on a collaborative mixed method participatory action research study. *Qualitative Health Research, 18*(5), 701–717.

Wiener, C. (1984) The burden of rheumatoid arthritis. In Strauss, A. (ed) *Chronic Illness and the Quality of Life.* St. Louis, MO: C. V. Mosby Co.

Worthington, C., & Myers, T. (2003). Factors underlying anxiety in HIV testing: Risk perceptions, stigma, and the patient-provider power dynamic. *Qualitative Health Research, 13*(5), 636–655.

Yan, M. C. (2002). *A grounded theory study on culture and social workers: Towards a dialectical model of cross-cultural social work.* Ottawa, Canada: National Library of Canada.

Yan, M. C. (2005). How cultural awareness works: An empirical examination of the interaction between social workers and their clients. *Canadian Social Work Review, 22*(1), 5–29.

Yan, M. C. (2008a). Exploring cultural tensions in cross-cultural social work practice. *Social Work, 53*(4), 317–328.

Yan, M. C. (2008b). Exploring the meaning of crossing and culture: An empirical understanding from practitioners' everyday experience. *Families in Society: The Journal of Contemporary Social Services, 89(2)*, 282–292. DOI:10.1606/1044-3894.3744.

Zimbalist, S. E. (1977). *Historic themes and landmarks in social welfare research.* New York, NY: Harper & Row.

Index

Note: Figures are indicated by *f.* Text boxes are indicated by *b.*

CPSIA information can be obtained at www.ICGtesting.com
Printed in the USA
BVOW021522171211

278625BV00006B/5/P